THE BATTLE FOR RHODESIA

The Battle for Rhodesia

by

DOUGLAS REED

P.O.BOX 1371 CAPE TOWN *1967*

Finally, brethren, whatsoever things are true, whatsoever things are honest, whatsoever things are just, whatsoever things are pure, whatsoever things are lovely, whatsoever things are of good report: if there be any virtue, and if there be any praise, think on these things.

These are the golden rules for a writer. The qualities enumerated are hard to find in the picture of our times, but I have tried to discern them as I went along and to give them their place in this chronicle of events as seen by me.

First Edition: August, 1966
Second Edition: September, 1966
Third Edition: September, 1966
Fourth Edition: October, 1966
Fifth Edition: October, 1966
Sixth Edition: November, 1966
Seventh Edition: December, 1966
Eighth Edition: January, 1967

First published by HAUM P.O. Box 1371 Cape Town
Printed by the Citadel Press Lansdowne

CONTENTS

Respected reader,

To those of you who know my books (a diminishing band: but aren't we all?) and to those who know them not, let me recall that in 1936, sitting at a window in Vienna, I wrote a book, *Insanity Fair*, about the coming Second World War. In 1966, sitting at a window in Salisbury, Rhodesia, I find myself writing this book about the coming of a Third World War. This is where we all came in. The scene has shifted from Europe to Africa, but the new post-war years have seen the same ladderlike process calculably leading to war.

In these latter years I did many things, and writing was of the things undone, for my writ, I felt, ran out. There was only the oft-told tale to re-tell and its constant iteration came too near the praising of myself, for every fool can play upon words. If "warnings" were needed, let others warn, and probably in vain, for by a divine instinct men's minds mistrust ensuing danger. So I sought other paths and spent many years in South Africa.

Man proposes: looking for pastures new, I found myself in the centre of another world conflict in the brewing. Africa was this time the scene of the preparatory steps, and Southern Africa the last rung of the war-ladder. The British Government's onslaught on Rhodesia, in 1965, returned the world to its plight of 1937, when war was two moves away and could yet have been averted by obvious countermoves.

Let me briefly recall those days to you, senior and junior classmates. From 1933 Hitler's patent intention to make war was foretold by all competent observers in Berlin. Even the date (about five years ahead) was accurately estimated, in its despatches to London, by the Berlin office of *The Times* (where I was a correspondent).

The London government, however, to the end encouraged Hitler on his warpath by the method called "appeasement" (throwing children to pursuing wolves until only the parents remain, in the fleeing sleigh, for the wolves to devour). German rearmament was let pass, then the seizure of the Rhineland, then the recreation of the German air force (in 1935 Hitler personally told the British Foreign Minister of its massive strength, as I then reported).

9

That left two pieces on the board, and they provided the final test. If Hitler kept within his frontiers, "appeasement" would be vindicated. If he forayed out of them, it would collapse and war follow. Seeking to reach the public mind, I wrote in *Insanity Fair* "Austria means you" and "Czechoslovakia means you".

Austria was invaded as the book appeared. One last move remained. If he were allowed to invade Czechoslovakia, world war was certain. I repeated this in a second book, *Disgrace Abounding*, and also opined that the Second War would begin with a Hitler-Stalin alliance.

Six months after the Austrian invasion, the British Prime Minister, from a meeting with Hitler, sent a timed ultimatum to the Czecho-slovak President to surrender his defensive zone. M. Benesh, saying "We bequeath our sorrows to the West", capitulated. Mr. Chamberlain, back in Downing Street, announced "Peace in our time". Hitler took the Czechoslovak defences, disclaimed any further "territorial demands", and six months later invaded the rest of Czechoslovakia. Six months after that, punctually to the foreseeable moment, the Second War began.

As the German tanks entered Prague, I left (as I left Vienna a year earlier, after telephonic warning from my London office that the Gestapo disliked me, which I knew). Soon I quitted journalism, too, for *Insanity Fair* was not popular with the highpriests of appeasement, a sacred word at that time. My editor, a Mr. Dawson, was a foremost advocate of it and told me "*Insanity Fair* is an excellent book, but not one for *The Times*" (I had submitted it before publication as in duty bound) so I resigned. (*The Times*, in its later *Official History*, confessed error about its policy of 1933–1939 and in the same breath unrepentantly sneered at "junior members of the staff" who resigned in protest. The *History* also admits that *The Times* had "abandoned the practice of basing a foreign policy of the paper's own upon the dispatches, published and private, of 'our own' Correspondents abroad". Had *The Times*, then a powerful force in the world, *maintained* that policy it could, in my judgment, have averted the Second War. Today, 1966, it still does not base policy on the information of trustworthy correspondents abroad: if it did, it could not support the policy pursued by British Governments in Africa since 1945, of destroying order in Africa and thus preparing new war. (Incidentally, the term "junior members", quoted above,

10

should be read in the singular: in fact the resigner was a singular person called Douglas Reed).

Insanity Fair, in 1938, gave a true picture of the wrath to come at a time when it could have been averted. It was simply prognostic and *not* "prophetic".

These are my credentials, good reader, for returning, in 1966, to write one more book. I have briefly retold the events of 1933–1939 in Europe to draw the comparison between them and those of 1960–1966 in Africa, and to say: "Rhodesia means you".

Ten years ago a major war beginning in Africa was inconceivable. While wars, "hot" and "cold", went on elsewhere, Africa was a continent of order. It was steadily moving to an improving future for all its peoples under the colonial powers, as they pursued the established policy of gradually uplifting the tribespeople towards an increasing part in the management of affairs. With folk separated by millennia from every "Western" concept, gradualism was the only method. Violent interruption of this process meant (as is now being seen) reversion to a chaotic tribalism of slavery, warfare and disease, the things of which Africa was slowly being purged.

Only one power in the world *admittedly* desired this. Lenin, in 1920, decreed that the expulsion of the colonial powers from their territories was vital to the achievement of world communism. In the years 1960–1966 Western "liberalism" openly supported this Leninist aim. This partnership, indeed, between the governments of the "free world" and communism, their professed enemy, is the basic fact of the years 1960–1966 in Africa. Only when that is understood does the picture of what has happened become plain, as a photograph emerges from a film in developing liquid.

The "wind of change" speech began it all. I see Mr. Macmillan now, mellifluously addressing the Cape Town Parliament. Icy rejection underlay the courtesy of the Afrikaner Members who listened, and their unspoken comment was, "Here we have it again: perfidy". I recall my own feeling that day: "This is Mr. Chamberlain again". I thought of the days, thirty years before, when British policy towards Hitler was formed by knickerbockered figures at country-house parties, during weekends on grouse moors or beside trout streams, in too-substantial midday meals at the Carlton and Athenaeum Clubs, far from the madding truth of events in Europe. Had any been there to watch, t'would have been pitiful to see me

11

wring my hands and murmur, Oh dearie, dearie me, here we go again.

The "wind of change" speech began the era of Doubletalk, the use of words to disguise, not express intention. These particular words suggested a natural process, uncontrollable by man: the wind bloweth where it listeth. They meant a political decision to abandon Africa to turbulence and war.

From that day fiasco followed on perfidy in Africa as if some grisly Quixote, followed by his Sancho Panza, rode on skeleton mounts through a dark vale of bones. The sudden change of policy was as if a good ship, built to ply the seas until in high old age it should be honourably consigned to the wreckers' yard, were scuttled in mid-ocean.

Almost at once Belgium, under the mysterious outside "pressure" which governs governments in our time, jettisoned the Congo, and for three years killing and rapine followed. Under American pressure, "United Nations" troops, now of unhallowed memory, were sent, not to preserve life or restore order, but to prevent the secession from chaos of its one orderly and well-governed province, Katanga, and to drive out the only black statesman produced by Africa until that time, M. Moise Tshombe.

The London government, under similar occult pressure, offered 1,000 lb. "blockbuster" bombs to help subdue Katanga and M. Tshombe. Rhodesia's Sir Roy Welensky redeemed the name of England at that moment by refusing to allow "the transit of bombs which we know are destined to be used against almost defenceless people who are fighting for their homeland, but who have ranged against them at least one of the great powers of the world today". Mr. Macmillan, when Sir Roy refused to withhold this statement, withheld the bombs. (This incident of blockbusters to be used "strictly for defensive purposes" against black people in the Congo is a classic example of Doubletalk).

After that the rot set in which, in the next five years, moved swiftly from the north of Africa southward, destroying the fabric of orderly development as white ants devour a good floor.

Ghana was then already independent and Nigeria followed at once. These were held up as the showpieces of Western-type, parliamentary government, successfully transplanted. In those two dark pools the Western "liberals" thought to see, Narcissus-like, their own fair reflection: blood had not yet surged across the surface, blotting out this illusion. They were given paper constitutions of the Western kind. Titles and orders of nobility were bestowed on their leaders. This was to be The New Commonwealth.

The destructive process quickened as one new "State" after another, lacking the resources or experience to qualify it for statehood, was hurled into independence. The vote-for-all, after one-vote-once, became a free-for-all. Massacre was followed by tribal wars (simmering beneath the surface during the period of colonial control, these revived when it was removed). One-party rule, military governments and dictatorships appeared on all hands, "Strong men" popped up and were ousted by other strong men, soon to be ousted. Foreseeably, "the army" took over in many places. "Army" does not mean, in Africa, what Western folk understand, with their mental images of West Point parades, Changing the Guard, or stomping Red Army masses. It means, the few men who have guns. Where no law runs, he with the gun prevails, as at Tombstone, for instance, in Wild West days.

The tribesman accepts strength as the ultimate. Force, deliberately used, is to him unanswerable: unintentionally used, it amuses him. I have seen a Zulu struck in the forehead by a cricket ball travelling at something near the speed of sound: whether he lived I know not, but his friends around laughed themselves into the ground.

Mrs. Dugauquier (*Congo Cauldron*) gives two illustrative examples. A silent film of the trial and execution of Jesus was shown in a Catholic Church to Congolese tribesmen. At the whipping, "excited cries of 'Pika!' Strike! rang out . . . quite naturally, as in a Western film we cheer on the goodies and boo the baddies, they were encouraging the strong against the weak". In another film, showing the white man's suppression of the Arab slave traders (their hereditary enemies), "each slash of the long whip on the wretched black man's back was cheered wholeheartedly" and when the rescuing white man was floored by the Arab slaver, "their shouts reached a crescendo of support for the Arab, not as representing a race, creed or idea, but simply because he symbolized power and force".

A Basuto chief, who impressed me by his authority, dignity, good English and knowledge of the great world, was later hanged for a ritual murder (a "strong medicine" killing: parts taken from the living victim, are used to reinforce a compound potent against spirits

13

hostile to the chief or the tribe). This was nothing personal against the chosen victim. The chief had no sense of wrongdoing, and the tribespeople (save possibly for the child victim's parents, and they would not dare protest) respected his motive and act.

In short, people are not only funny but different, and the hundreds of tribes now more or less "represented" by the 35 or 36 new African "States" at the United Nations were truly not ready for the responsibilities thrust upon them.

However, these new apprentices, with the support of what is called "the Afro-Asian bloc" and of the Soviet group, acquired a majority at the United Nations. In December 1965 this combine voted out the rule about important issues requiring a two-thirds majority and changed it to simple majority. By that time the London and Washington governments were on the verge of using force to compel "one-man-one-vote", with the same foreseeable result, in the small remaining area of orderly government in Africa. They appeared constantly to retreat before the demands of the newly-created majority in the United Nations, where Togo (population 1,500,000) had about 175 times the voting power of the United States (population 180,000,000): yet these governments must have foreseen what would happen in New York when they brought into being this new voting-mass.

The new "States", inevitably, began to clamour for their powerful godparents, in London and Washington, to use "force", for, as I have shown, force is the thing they understand, and they could by this time count on a majority, artificially created, at the United Nations for any warmongering. By this means they did, in 1966, bring the world to the very verge of another world war, and the danger is not past.

There remained only, in 1966, as the last bulwark of order in Africa, the last dam against the waters of chaos, South Africa, Rhodesia and the two Portuguese territories, Mozambique and Angola. Punctually to the moment, a sound like that of jackals in the African night arose from the building on East 42nd Street, as the new "majority" imperiously demanded that war be made against Rhodesia, which stood between them and their supporting cohorts of "Western liberalism" and the real target, South Africa.

The war they wanted was to be waged, not by them, but by Britain and America. These two countries, by their actions between

14

1960 and 1965, gave enough cause to fear that they might do even this bidding.

At that moment in the debacle Rhodesia declared independence and opposed itself to the outer world gone mad. Two sentences from Mr. Ian Smith's independence day speech leaped at me when I heard them: "To us has been given the privilege of being the first Western nation in the last two decades to have the determination and fortitude to say, 'So far and no further' . . . We may be a small country but we are a determined people who have been called upon to play a role of worldwide significance".

Was it possible, I thought, that at last a country, this little country in Africa, would oppose itself to the Gadarene process of these last three decades (I would say three, not two: because all this began in the Thirties)? Might one still hope that the rot would be stemmed, the destructive process held and turned back? To me, more perhaps than to any other hearer, Mr. Ian Smith's words fell into the context of world events stretching back to 1933 and into a historical perspective of my own experience.

For I saw Austria and Czechoslovakia fall. They would have resisted if they could, but the foe was too close and mighty, and all their friends false. Now Rhodesia was in their plight, and faced a world entire of foes bent on its destruction for a purpose further beyond.

If this wonder could happen, I knew, if Rhodesia *could* in fact stand fast and hold out and win, the prospect for all our tomorrows would vastly change and improve.

Thus, dear reader, that busy little bee your humble servant, having watched what brewed from South Africa for many years, went to Rhodesia to watch the outcome of this epic struggle, for on it depended the future: chaos in all Africa and general war; or stability restored in Africa and peace in Africa, at least for some time yet.

Rhodesia means you, good people, as Austria and Czechoslovakia meant you. This is a warning book about a coming Third World War. So was *Insanity Fair*, in 1938. Now, as then, it need not happen, and that is why I have written. Room and time remain to avoid war, in 1966 as in 1938. Had Hitler been stopped at the gates of Austria and Czechoslovakia in 1938, no Second War would have occurred. If simple reason prevails, and Rhodesia survives, there will be no

Third World War, beginning in Africa: those who desire one will have to look elsewhere for a pretext.

It is simple enough, a mathematical calculation. Rhodesia means you, from Whitehall to Washington, Wisconsin to Worcestershire, Wigan to Wilmington and Winnipeg, and you cannot escape it. Rhodesia is no distant, isolated African episode: it reaches into your very home, however far away you be.

And now, good companions, let us look at this "little country far away, that we know nothing about": Rhodesia.

In 1890 the American frontier halted. The last Indian hunting-grounds were overrun and the Redskins (in Canada too) left in enclaves similar to South Africa's "Bantustans" of today, (save that these are to become self-governing states).

In Africa the moving frontier went on moving. In both places the pattern was the same: the horsedrawn covered wagons and the oxen-drawn trek wagons formed laagers when the attack came: Custer's Last Stand of 1878 and Major Alan Wilson's last stand of 1893 alike left no white man alive. Destiny was "manifest" in each case and "pioneer" was a brave name.

It was an old name, too, for pioneering began four hundred years earlier, when Bartholomew Diaz reached and Vasco da Gama rounded the Cape. The seas were uncharted and their seamen feared to fall off the edge of the world. Da Gama's feat of seamanship in reaching and planting the Cross on Natal's shore on Christmas Day 1498 (hence "Natal", for the Nativity) in his wooden cockleshell was great, for these are treacherous waters where even in the 1960's big steel vessels such as the *Aimèe Lykes*, may strike the shoals. Then in 1652 Jan van Riebeeck was left at the Cape to store water and grow vegetables for Dutch ships eastward bound, and out of this market-garden sprang a new nation, Afrikanerdom, now a growing moral force in the world.

In 1776 the American colonists proclaimed their independence of government from three thousand miles away. The word "colonialism" then meant this mismanagement by remote control: today the word has been turned upside down and is used as a reproach against government-on-the-spot.

The Boers followed the American example when the Dutch ceded the Cape to England in 1806. They too, could not endure the distant hand and proclaimed UDI in their own way: they inspanned their wagons, trekked over the northward mountains and across the Orange and Vaal, and set up their own republics. Therewith the moving frontier moved far inland and with the Portuguese settlements on the western and eastern coasts, Southern Africa became the white man's settled domain.

Remained the unknown middle part of Africa, a dark enigma,

and soon the moving frontier moved thither. Into that unknown land, in the 1840's and later, came first the missionaries, led by those great Scotsmen Robert Moffat, his son-in-law David Livingstone, John Moffat, James Stewart and others. The world hailed them, too, as Christian pioneers, and America shared the sense of pride when the Britisher, Henry Morton Stanley (late of the U.S. Navy), sent by Gordon Bennett and the *New York Herald* to search for Livingstone, found him in 1871.

Even today Central Africa is a formidable place and the dangers these men endured, though different, were not less than those braved by those later pioneers, the astronauts of today. Slave raids and inter-tribal wars, wild beasts and reptiles, malaria, dysentery, blackwater fever, yaws, Little Irons: all these made for nightmare journeys and the men who achieved them were held in the awe that is the due of Spacemen now.

The world they left behind was solidly with them, for their great purpose was to root out slavery, which the warrior tribes and the Arab slave-traders together practised. They were the banner-bearers of Christian civilization in Central Africa, and all Europe and America, in that Victorian heyday, shared this belief. So did the "settlers" who followed.

From the day when Livingstone, seeking the source of the Nile, discovered the Thundering Smoke (Victoria Falls) and went on to explore the Zambezi River, the frontier began to move northward again, into what is today Rhodesia. Its original peoples, the Bushmen and Hottentots, had been exterminated by warrior tribes and the area now was held by later comers, the newly-arrived Matabele in the west and the Mashona in the east. The Matabele, under King Moselikatze, some decades earlier split off and fled from the Zulus of Natal, under the terrible Chaka. They were warriors and scorned the Mashona "dogs". (After seventy years of the white man's peace this feud still simmers and would at once burst out if one-man-one-vote were imposed here, for the Mashona are far more numerous than the Matabele, who would not submit to this "majority rule": for this reason both groups want the white man's protection to continue).

Into this dangerous scene stepped a clergyman's son from England, Cecil Rhodes, who by 1878 gained control of the Kimberley diamond industry. His vision went beyond money and a diamond empire. His conviction was that the white man was best fitted to open up Central Africa, the dark enigma. Like Livingstone, he believed that white enterprise alone could save the continent from poverty, slavery and disease and that British rule would be a blessing for its peoples. Britain, he held, could not afford to stand aloof: without her overseas possessions the little kingdom would be but an overcrowded, insignificant island in northern European waters. Today his belief is receiving its ultimate test (and you, dear insular reader, will see the answer).

Rhodes looked northward, wondering if another gold and diamond empire might lie in the land that now bears his name. In 1888 John Moffat obtained from King Lobengula, Moselikatze's successor, the concession of "all metals and minerals" in the Matabele Kingdom for Rhodes and his "British South Africa Company". In 1889 Queen Victoria signed the Charter empowering the Company, in effect, to govern the territory.

Next came the task of moving the frontier across the territory thus assigned, where were only a tiny handful of white men, isolated among Lobengula and his redoubtable impis and the Mashona. Rhodes formed the Pioneer Corps of some 200 picked men, accompanied by 500 British South Africa Company police*. This column succeeded in by-passing the hostile Matabele and on September 12, 1890 reached the spot which they called Fort Salisbury: the beleaguered Salisbury of today.

With that the moving frontier halted and the white man established himself in the land. The Pioneers ("duke's son, cook's son . . .") dispersed and were given mining claims and farms. Among them was an American, William Harvey Brown. He called his farm Arlington (after Arlington, D.C.) and travellers landing at Salisbury Airport today alight on its site.

The white man was in Rhodesia but three wars had to be fought before he was secure. King Lobengula had agreed that he might mine for gold, but the Matabele warriors did not agree that they must cease from enslaving the Mashona, who in turn deduced that the white man was too weak to protect them and refused labour for his mines and farms. In 1893 Mashona were massacred near Fort

*The British South Africa police have retained the name and still keep order in Rhodesia today. This is an élite force with a magnificent tradition, comparable with the Mounties of Canada and the Texas Rangers.

Victoria and when the Matabele king refused to give up his claim to the Mashona raiding grounds, war began. Lobengula burned his capital and fled. Major Alan Wilson with a small force tried to capture Lobengula in his kraal and failed: all were wiped out. Lobengula escaped and died, possibly by suicide, Matabele resistance collapsed, and in later time a great city, Bulawayo, rose on the site of Lobengula's kraal.

After that the number of settlers quickly increased, but in 1895 the collapse of Dr. Jameson's raid into the Transvaal, which dimmed Rhodes's prestige, and the consequent absence of white troops from Matabeleland, again persuaded the Matabele that the white man could be crushed: he was weak! They rose in 1896 in the usual manner: 130 unsuspecting white men and their families were shot, stoned, bludgeoned or speared. A force of 2,000 white and 600 black troops was raised to put down this rising but (as in the later South African war) an elusive enemy, fighting on his home ground of precipitous kopjes, rocks, boulders and caves, proved hard to find and fight.

Then the Mashona, of whom the white folk had adopted the Matabele's opinion, surprised all by rising too. They also thought the white man was weak, that the Matabele would win, and that they, the Mashona, would pay the price if they did not help crush the white man. Their rising followed the Matabele pattern: servants thought faithful suddenly turned and did women and children to death, murdered prospectors in their camps, miners in their shafts, storekeepers behind their counters. (In the 1960's this pattern was often repeated, in Kenya, the Congo and other newly "independent" places: the old ways reappeared).

The Mashona were subdued in 1897. In the meantime Rhodes performed his legendary exploit of pacifying the fierce Matabele. With a small, unprotected party, including two women, he met the Matabele chiefs and induced them to lay down their arms. They gave him the name "Lamula 'mkunzi", "Separator of the Fighting Bulls", for this, his greatest triumph. This, the start of seventy years of peace, is today a memory as vivid and significant in the Matabele and Mashona mind as that of Magna Charta or Independence in the British and American one. For them, a new life began that day.

(Seventy years later, a Mr. Arthur Bottomley from Walthamstow met the Matabele and Mashona chiefs, to whom Rhodes and his achievement were a living memory, as they repeatedly told him. He could not at all grasp the significance of the episode: they found him unintelligible; and although the African chief is a model of courtesy in such debates, one of them in despair was moved to say, "If I had my own way we would walk out of this meeting and leave Mr. Bottomley here alone". Kipling was right: when two strong men stand face to face they can understand each other, no matter what their skin or language. Between such as Mr. Bottomley and these tribal leaders no communion of minds was possible. Across the great gulf fixed between them, the chiefs looked and saw the living emblem of the white man's weakness, to them the fault beyond forgiving).

The two rebellions cost the whites about one-tenth of their numbers in casualties, a percentage, I believe, never otherwise known in war. The white folk never faltered or thought of quitting. They stayed and (as Mr. L. H. Gann says*) "Their will to rule remained unbroken. They felt that history was on their side, that Europe stood behind them, and that they formed the vanguard of civilization in Darkest Africa . . . The whites in Rhodesia never experienced that clammy sense of moral and political isolation, which weighed down their successors two generations later".

That means today. If "history" is that which is manufactured in our time by machines that reach the ear, eye and mind of millions, then it *is* against the whites. But they still believe what their grandparents believed. When a British Minister told Rhodesian representatives. "We have lost the will to govern", one of them told him "But we have not". In Rhodesia, and in South Africa, the white man's will still "remains unbroken" for a' that, no matter what may happen in Rhodes's overcrowded little island in the North Sea or elsewhere.

The moving frontier halted at last, in 1897, seven years after the American one stopped. Followed seventy years during which no black man needed fear the slave-raiders or the outcry of enemy tribes in the night, around his huts. There was peace in the land.

Today the attempt is to destroy all that thus was gained.

*In his classic *History of Southern Rhodesia*, Chatto & Windus, 1965.

In the haste of writing this book, I over-compressed the events outlined in the second paragraph of page 19, and did less than justice to one of two brave men. John Moffat, at Rhodes's instigation, played a great part in securing the preliminary treaty, but the galant C.D. Rudd secured the final concession, which bears his name.

21

In following years the territory encompassed by the moving frontier was divided into three parts: Southern and Northern Rhodesia (effectively governed by the Company) and Nyasaland (governed directly from London). Between 1900 and 1910 slavery and tribal wars were stamped out in all.

Southern Rhodesia (today's Rhodesia), the area of the original conquest, was a case by itself. Its white population was greater and its development quicker: the African bushveld began to blossom like the rose; and the settlers grew restive under the hand of a board of directors in London, as the American colonists, earlier, under that of King George. As the date for the renewal of the Company's charter from the Queen approached, their demand for self-government swelled. In 1922 the voters were offered, by referendum, self-government or (at Mr. Winston Churchill's suggestion) union with South Africa. Much talk of a republic was heard from South Africa and the Rhodesians, intensely loyal to The Crown, chose Responsible Government, which London granted in 1923.

Rhodes was dead, but his work flourished. From that day, 43 years ago, Rhodesia has governed itself, London retaining only some control over laws affecting the tribal population and safeguarding them against any discriminatory disabilities. The successive Constitutions have contained no racial discrimination. The qualification for the vote requires moderate amounts in cash, property or income.

In practice the black community votes little, for reasons which lengthy residence among them alone can make clear. Most of them find "voting" unintelligible: their immemorial tradition is against "choosing" and for decisions reached in pyramidal tribal conclave of villagers, village elders, district headmen and chiefs. The notion that "the children", at the bottom level, should challenge tribal authority and unanimity is as Chinese to them. They believe that the tribe's spirits, or ancestors, consulted through the chief's medium, or oracle, ultimately decide the tribe's weal or woe.

For example: in one tribe a child was sacrificed, at the spirit's bidding, to the rain-god. The Chief was imprisoned for eighteen months and on the day of his release rain fell. The tribespeople drew the obvious conclusion (incidentally, their beliefs are respected by white folk who *live* among them).

Again, the educated and well-to-do African townsman, with a business, remains subject to his tribe's communal custom of sharing possessions. If a man has six wives and sixty-one children, (a case known to me), he well may not wish to declare even the modest amount of property qualifying him for a vote.

Time and patient responsible statesmanship might in time produce a harmonious solution to the most difficult problem of the world. Only an irresponsible interruption, engineered from outside, can endanger that. The British Socialist Party, founded in 1900, never yet obtained a majority of *votes*, yet it seeks to force the dogma of "black majority rule" into Africa's resistant soil, which is like trying to grow cokernuts in Camberwell.

The only statesmanlike leader yet produced by that party, Mr. Clement Attlee, in 1952 told one of the now-now politicos from Northern Rhodesia, "You have a long way to go in this field: look how long it took our British Parliament to achieve fully responsible government". To Mr. Nkumbula's reply, "We have received guidance, we can reach political maturity in much less time", Mr. Attlee rejoined, "I don't think you are right on that point. Constitutional government can't be learned from textbooks. You're trying to rush things. My experience has taught me that it takes a long time to get a democratic idea working effectively".

Had Mr. Attlee's successors been men of such balance, the world would not find "Rhodesia" in the headlines every day. Statesmanship takes time. Given time, it works: denied time, all falls into a smouldering shambles that can only be kept down by the lid of force. This result has been seen everywhere in Africa where Britain and America have "tried to rush things".

I discussed these things with African leaders of the opposition in and out of Parliament, and also with Chiefs and tribesmen in the tribal districts and the towns. The political gentlemen were against gradualness and for immediacy (black majority rule now): what political gentleman would not be, with great outside powers threatening to bring the world in arms to enforce everything-now and all-at-once.

The Chiefs were strongly for orderly development which to them meant peace in their districts. The man-in-the-kraal took

23

guidance from them. As to the African man-in-the-street, I quote a French journalist, with an interpreter, who once stopped the first black man he saw in a Salisbury street and asked whether he wanted the white folk to stay or go. To stay, the man answered. Why, asked the Frenchman. "If you had been here last year" (1964, the time of the killings and burnings by communist-trained terrorists from outside) "you would not ask", said the man, "we want them to protect us".

Gradualism produced results, in the form of increasing African* participation in Parliament and all walks of life. However, gradualism, though the best expedient now and for the near future, is *not* a solution. The solution, as I will later show, lies elsewhere.

In thirty years of self-government, 1923–1953, Rhodesia strode ahead as if on seven-league boots. The astonishing thing is how much was done in how short a time. That impressed me in South Africa, too, but South Africa has a white population of some millions and has had three centuries to build. Rhodesia has a white population of about a quarter-million and has had but seventy years.

At the start the land was scrub, constantly impoverished by the tribal method of farming and by erosion. The lifegiving waters drained away into the Indian Ocean. Disease, tribal raids and wild beasts ravaged the people and the land. It was still, as James Stewart found it in the 1860's, "a lonely land of barbarism, of wild beasts, of timid and harried but not unkindly men, harassed by never-ending slave raids and inter-tribal wars".

Today water conservation in Rhodesia is a model for the world. The lethal diseases, killing and slavery have been stamped down and almost out. The white farming areas show crops, the equal of those in the Mid West or anywhere in the world. The tribes occupy more than half the land, but the contribution of this to the economy is insignificant because the tribesman clings to his immemorial custom of growing just enough to eat, grazing the land bare, and when it is denuded, breaking up his huts and moving elsewhither, there to repeat the process.

The allegation is often heard that the tribes "only get the poorest land". The matter may be checked, by any who care, at the great

---

*I dislike to use this misleading word: white Rhodesians and South Africans, of two, three or more generations in the land, are as much "Africans" as any black folk. However, in today's idiom its use seems unavoidable to describe a man of black pigmentation.

24

Triangle sugarlands in the Rhodesian lowveld. This land was raw scrub in 1912 and little that looked less promising could have been found when another indomitable Scotsman, Tom MacDougall, saw it then. The First War delayed him but in 1919 he began with his hands to clear a patch or two. A secondhand mill, bought in Natal, needed two years to reach him, by lorry and ox-wagon, from the border at Beit Bridge. By 1935 he produced ten tons of sugar. Today, when big concerns have taken over, twenty thousand acres are under sugar and the endless crops gladden the eye of man.

The land problem may be studied at the Domboshawa Training Centre, near Salisbury, where men from the tribal districts receive instruction in local self-government. It was formerly an agricultural training centre and still has a farm, where fine crops grow. On the other side of its fence is tribal land, bare and denuded, where, one might say, nothing would grow. The land on either side of the fence is the same: only the method is different.

The white man's achievement may be studied, for example, in little Umtali, which reminded me of a mountain village in the Blue Ridge Mountains. It has 9,000 white and 35,000 black people, and the white ones provide nine-tenths of its revenue. Over the years this small place has built some six thousand houses for the African community and (from beer-hall proceeds) a stadium for the black folk costing £75,000, a swimming pool, picture-theatre, infant schools and crèches and much more. I doubt whether an English or American town of comparable size could equal this achievement.

Rhodesia's growth was always fast but the great acceleration came after the Second War, in 1945. The next twenty years brought probably the most rapid development the world has ever seen. Still building on the tradition of sound administration and probity in public affairs which it thought to be its rocklike heritage from England, the country flourished exceedingly, managing its own affairs and spending nobody's money but its own.

Within Rhodesia the people, white and black, grew in beauty, as one might say, side by side. The emphasis is on *side by side*, as distinct from together, and here lies the difference between the temporary expedient, gradualism, and the ultimate solution, separateness.

Before Responsible Government was granted in 1923 the

Rhodesian delegates in London raised the question of territorial segregation and Mr. Winston Churchill (then the Minister competent) agreed that the existing law might be changed if an impartial enquiry upheld this method. Seldom was so emphatic a judgment delivered as that of the Commission then appointed (under Sir Morris Carter):

"The evidence . . . leaves no doubt as to the wishes *of all classes of the inhabitants* . . . an *overwhelming majority* of those who understand the question are in favour of the establishment of *separate areas* in which each of the two races, black and white, should be permitted to acquire interests in land . . . However desirable it may be that members of the two races should live together side by side with equal rights as regards the holding of land, we are convinced that in practice, probably for generations to come, such a policy is not practicable or in the best interests of the two races. Until the Native has advanced very much further on the paths of civilization it is better that the points of contact between the two races should be reduced and a lengthy period afforded for the study of the whole question of the future of the relations between the two races in an atmosphere which is freed as far as possible from the setbacks which would ensue from the irritations and conflicts arising from the constant close proximity of members of races of different habits, ideals and outlook upon life" (my italics).

This was then, and today is the immutable African truth, unpalatable to those who live snug, and perhaps smug, on Boston's Back Bay or Bournemouth's beachfront, and very anathema to those high initiates who seek through chaos in Africa to set up the World Dictatorship. Wisdom spoke then. Today, the pressure, and the menaces, from London and Washington are used to enforce the very opposite of this prudent ruling, to exacerbate "irritations and conflicts", to set the two races against each other, and to foment an atmosphere of war.

But if the future is to be one of improving relationship between white and black folk, and of mutual betterment in material things, separate life in separate lands is the only longterm solution. In Rhodesia policy followed this recommendation and the white and black areas are distinct, but dotted in enclaves over the map. What the chief and tribesman most would like would be a separate homeland, side by side with a white homeland, in Rhodesia, and for this reason he gazes approvingly across the frontier at the Transkei, South Africa's first "Bantustan".

The end of the Second War and the great boom which followed gave impetus to an idea, long discussed, for closer union between Rhodesia (then Southern Rhodesia) and its two neighbours, Northern Rhodesia and Nyasaland. Together, these would have provided a hard core of political stability, and a great source of common wealth, in the heart of Africa. Out of this came conferences in 1949 and 1951, when the British and the three territorial governments together drafted a scheme for a Federation "which would be a much-needed stabilizing factor in a continent which is in such a state of flux". The Southern Rhodesian Prime Minister of that time, Sir Godfrey Huggins, said, "It is up to us to save Central Africa by our exertions and Africa by our example".

Of all sad words . . . In 1953 the great Federation of the two Rhodesias and Nyasaland was set up, and a splendid future opened for Central Africa. The London government, as now transpires, at that time was already set on a course which could only worsen Africa's "state of flux" into a state of shambles. Within ten years the British Government destroyed the Federation created by it and all Africa was deprived of the gyrostabilizer in its central hold.

Let us now take a look at those years of Doubletalk which left Rhodesia alone in a world determined to incite its races against each other.

As to that, there is one simple test by which the white folk's supreme achievement in Rhodesia, in relation to the black ones, may be measured. If life be the greatest gift of all, then the white man gave the black one life. Seventy years ago some 400,000 tribespeople occupied this area, and but for the coming of the white man they would not be many more today: disease, the assegai and the slaver would have seen to that. Today they number over 4,000,000, half of them children. They have been rid of disease, infant mortality, death by the spear and burning, and abduction and sale to the bordellos and harems of Arabia.

THE DECADE OF DOUBLETALK

The Federation began like a rising sun. Three territories, separately small, by joining their resources formed a great union with a productive capacity enough to ensure the betterment of all its peoples. Investment money and immigrants poured in, and, symbol of the brightening future, an old dream was at once realized: the Kariba Dam was built to store the Zambezi's waters and fructify the lands on either side and far beyond.

This hope and confidence were in fact illusory, for the Federation rested on two buttresses, one in London and one in Rhodesia, of which the London one was a hollow sham. The compact between both parties there, to abandon the African possessions, already existed, and that inevitably meant wrecking the Federation and producing a war situation in Africa: the years have shown this. For a decade the Rhodesian leaders struggled against what they thought was delusion in London but in truth was resolve. At the end they found themselves on the ruins of Federation and facing a levelled gun.

Quickly, then, the sunburst paled as the years of doubletalk followed, when the Rhodesian leaders tried to sink anchors into the pledges and assurances of London and found no hold. Sir Roy Welensky's tale of these 4,000 *Days* shows the development to a high art of the use of words to confuse and confound all who sought to cash them at face value. Sir Roy and his men, struggling to pierce this mass of wordage, passed from trust through perplexity to dazed unbelief and at last gave up, defeated.

The process gave a new word to the Barotse people (who were among the black folk sacrificed to the dogma of "black majority rule"): "ku-makmirana". Its definition, according to their Litunga, is "to discuss at great length and get nowhere: from the English Makmirana, or Macmillan". This way of employing speech now seems to have become general British usage (new in the West, that is: it is ancient in the Orient).*

*The African Chairman of the "Anti-Colonial Committee" of the United Nations in 1965 complained that the British delegate, after urging him privately to vote one way, himself voted the other way. Being told, "There should not be the slightest suspicion of any attempt to mislead you", he replied that his knowledge of English (which is excellent) was not such that he could understand all the fine shadings: "British delegates are resourceful in the use of words".

When the decade of decadence began, the phrases "Safe as the Bank of England", "A.1 at Lloyds" and "An Englishman's word is his bond" were as the law and the prophets to folk of British stock in Southern Africa. The Afrikaner's cold disbelief and the Frenchman's talk of Albion's perfidy brought smiles: they did not understand Us. I saw the British in Rhodesia and Natal, where they were predominant and devotedly loyal, gradually veer during this decade to the Afrikaner's side in distrust of London government. Inwardly they remained true to the ancient Crown and the British heritage as *they* understood it, but when menaces against themselves were put in the mouth of the Crown's wearer they feared that the ultimate intent must be to degrade or even destroy the monarchy, for such things seemed to them to deprive the concept of "constitutional monarchy" of meaning.

The fiasco of the Federation was in truth ordained before it was born, for in 1948 Sir Roy Welensky, canvassing support in London for an amalgamation of the two Rhodesias, was told by both Socialist and Conservative spokesmen that no government, of whichever party, would ever consider placing the control of the black folk in the hands of the fewer whites. This *was* the existing situation, and no public statement of its abandonment was ever made. Therefore the future deed was already foreseen.

However, at that point Sir Roy was put off the scent by a hint that "some form of federation" might be acceptable: and conferences between 1949 and 1953 hammered out the framework of a federation of the two Rhodesias and of little Nyasaland. By that time the Mau Mau killings had shown the indifferent world the facts of life in Africa, and a foremost authority, Lord Salisbury, said, "If England abandons these Central African territories they will go straight back to the conditions in which we found them, until they are gobbled up by people far less enlightened than ourselves". The years have shown and will show the truth of this.

Obviously the Federation, if it were to be set up at all, had to be built to last, or have that appearance. Lord Swinton (Commonwealth Secretary) said he knew of no federal constitution anywhere that contained a secession clause (save, he added smiling, in the Soviet Union). The Federation would need loans, and could never raise a penny if its continuance were in doubt. Mr. Lyttelton (Colonial Secretary: during the decade the harassed Rhodesians had to struggle with two distinct departments of State in the distant government) concurred, adding that they must have "legal assurance that the Federation could not be dissolved without the consent of *all* governments engaged". (Lord Swinton agreed, but commented, prophetically, that "You cannot legislate against the United Kingdom Government going off its head").

On this basis the Federation of the Rhodesias and Nyasaland was born in September 1953. Within it Southern Rhodesia was fully self-governing, as for thirty years: the other territories remained protectorates of the Crown. A review conference was foreseen in about ten years, but *not* (said London) "to decide whether Federation has succeeded or failed, or should be abolished or continued": it would merely recommend "such alterations as experience of its work has shown to be necessary during the first decade of its life".

The decade was to see many strange things. As it began the Korean war ended. It was supposedly waged against Chinese Communist aggression, yet Presidents Roosevelt and Truman, through General Marshall, set up Communism in China. The American commander was not allowed to win that war, which ended (like the Second War in Europe) in partition, the most fertile source of new war. America's part in world affairs became another riddle inside a mystery within an enigma. The great Republic stood fast, in words, against Communism, but, by deeds, showed growing hostility to countries which repressed Communism in their territories. And during this fateful decade America's mystifying presence began to be felt *in Africa*.

After three years came the Suez debacle, and London began to peel off its African possessions as at a clearance sale. Westminster-type paper constitutions were bestowed on them and Socialist politicians agitated loudly for the Federation to receive one patterned on that of Ghana (the working results of which have now been seen). In 1960 Mr. MacMillan, in Africa, announced his "wind of change" and British newspapers immediately claimed that this meant the end of the Federation, in the sense that any of its members now were free to secede.

Like hounds unleashed by these encouragements, "African nationalist leaders" (as the press called them) thronged to London, vociferating for "independence now" and were courted and fêted there as the voice of Africa. The Conservative government gazed, not at Africa, but at the next by-election, where the Socialists beat the big tomtom of "independence now": and the Socialists, when they came to office, would gaze, not at Africa, but at their own left-wingers, clamouring for "independence now". Chaos in Africa was being made on the British hustings. "Black majority rule" was a vote-getting slogan from London's slums to Manchester's suburbs (as was "Chinese slavery in Africa" sixty years before). Lenin's plan for Africa was being realized in London.

In 1960 Belgium overnight abandoned the Congo, which fell into chaos. Troops from various distant lands, with "U.N." painted on their helmets, arrived to prevent the secession of Katanga (no "secession" there!). These men, and their countries, had no conceivable interest in the Congo and, as they were paid, might be considered mercenaries. Those who were called "mercenaries" were a handful of fighters, mostly from Southern Africa, to whom most of the white hostages rescued owed their lives.

By 1960 the London government's actions, after Suez, had released a tide from the north which menaced the Federation. Katanga bordered it and thousands of refugees crossed into Northern Rhodesia. The involvement of Britain and America in the Congolese fiasco brought not only danger to the Federation but peril of general war: American troopcarriers were used against Katanga and the "defensive bombs" from Britain were withheld only at the last moment. The world, in 1960, was again very near a brink.

Thus the Federation was in a closing cage as the time for the "review" approached. In Northern Rhodesia and Nyasaland the "African nationalists" began by terrorism to force London's hand: any move to put them down was checked and rebuked by London. The Nyasaland Governor, at one point, was forced to use police and troops, and an investigating Commission (appointed at the instance of the clamorous African nationalists and their Socialist friends in London) found that he had so to act "or abdicate". The London Government's choice was the same, and its decision was already plain: abdication.

The Conservative government, ever in retreat before the sound and fury of the Opposition and the "African nationalists", then appointed a Royal Commission, under Lord Monckton, to enquire into conditions in the Federation. This obviously supplanted the Review Conference originally foreseen, which was committed to "no secession": once more the ulterior intention showed through the verbiage. Sir Roy Welensky said that if all that was needed to produce a Royal Commission was to stage a riot, the future was dark. He was soothed with a syrup of words: it would not be like that at all. Well then, asked the Rhodesians, suspicious but still loath to suspect, "what are to be the terms of reference?" Mr. Macmillan, in an exquisite exercise in phraseology, told the House of Commons:

"I regard the Commission as free in practice to hear all points of view from whatever quarter and on whatever subject . . . it is never wise to be too specific or rigid in interpretation . . . the terms of reference . . . include a very wide possibility for Lord Monckton and his colleagues to conduct their affairs in such a way as to bring about the result we all wish . . ." and so on and so on.

Sir Roy urgently asked what was this result so devoutly desired and Mr. Macmillan said he had "not yielded and would not yield an inch on the Commission's terms of reference." These, according to his statement quoted above, were elastic enough to stretch to infinity, so that an inch was of little moment, but Sir Roy still struggled to get down to brass tacks. Were the terms of reference to include *secession?* If so, he referred Mr. Macmillan to his pledge of April 27, 1957. Mr. Macmillan emphatically assured him that the British Government would *not* include secession in the terms of reference. Sir Roy so informed Rhodesia. Lord Shawcross, a member of the Royal Commission, then announced that he felt "completely free to entertain the views of any people on the whole future of the Federation". Mr. Macmillan, arrived in Salisbury, told indignant Rhodesian Ministers that he had been misunderstood by English newspapers which reported him as pledging "no forcible federation in Rhodesia". "I was not", he said, "referring at all to the possibility of secession from the Federation".

By this time it was clear that, in fact, the British Government would permit, and even prompt the two lesser members of the Federation to claim their Unilateral Declaration of Independence, but the game of words went on. Back in London, Mr. Macmillan ordered the release of Dr. Hastings Banda, then under detention on security grounds after the violent disturbances in Nyasaland. This was to the African nationalists the familiar "sign of weakness" and even louder uproar at once broke out.

To the very last the Rhodesian leaders thought that truth and the

pledged word were somewhere to be found, if they could only dis-
cover where, and they burrowed on. They invited Lord Home
(Commonwealth Secretary) to Salisbury and once more were engulfed by words:

"It is not inconceivable that, in the hypothetical event of an overwhelming volume of evidence being in favour of secession, the
Commission may have to consider whether, in fact, it can report
within its terms of reference or whether it may not have to say that
it is unable to report."

The efforts of Sir Roy and his weary men to get to grips with
their problem during all the years are wondrous to behold. Ever
and again they thought they knew which thimble contained the pea
and always they were wrong. The Monckton Commission next
recommended that "the British Government should declare its
intention of permitting secession" (UDI). However, the Commis-
sioners "regarded with concern" the possibility of the Federation's
break-up, now that they broke it up, and hoped that, given proper
safeguards, a right of secession might prove a "valuable safety
valve", and far from weakening the Federation might enable it to
survive. This is Parkinson's theory of seacocks, that the more water
is let in, the likelier the ship is to remain afloat.

After "this terrible piece of high explosive" was dropped from
London into Salisbury, Sir Roy reminded Mr. Macmillan of all
the pledges given between 1952 and 1959, and culminating in the
Governor General's Speech from the Throne even in 1960, stating
that secession was *not* to be considered by the Monckton Commission. Mr. Macmillan replied that the matter was indeed very
delicate and difficult and Sir Roy again felt himself enveloped "by
clouds of chilly cotton wool". He then hastened to London, to be
confronted by Mr. Macmillan, Mr. Duncan Sandys (Commonwealth Secretary), Mr. Ian Macleod (Colonial Secretary) and "a
huge array of African nationalists", and listened to "many hours of
their oratory with all its prejudice, racial hatred, special pleading
and demand for immediate and total political power". Then all
were taken for the familiar "full treatment" of a weekend at
Chequers, where Messrs. Kaunda and Banda demanded the
immediate dissolution of the Federation, and Sir Roy asked bluntly
if the British Government intended to destroy it. He could obtain
no answer but was wished a happy Christmas and safe journey home.

33

All was over but a little more doubletalk. Two months later the "Commonwealth Prime Ministers" (by this time including many new, "emergent" personages) met in London and forced the withdrawal of South Africa by the methods which thenceforth provided a majority for any irresponsible warcry from the "United Nations". In February 1962 Mr. Sandys personally conveyed to Sir Roy Dr. Banda's demand for Nyasaland's secession, and being told that a firm exercise of authority would keep Nyasaland peacefully in the Federation, replied (says Sir Roy), "No, you see, we British have lost the will to govern".* Sir Roy says this incident left him with a severe migraine and the British High Commissioner in Salisbury went home and vomited.

In London, at last, the two departments, Commonwealth and Colonial, were combined under a single Minister, Mr. R. A. B. Butler, who for thirty years looked like the next Conservative Prime Minister but was not destined to reach that office. The wonder is that he now undertook the executioner's task, and the strong possibility is that he did not know the purpose for which he would be used. This is indicated by the fact that in July 1962, when the Federation had but nine months to live, Mr. Butler, speaking in London, in specific terms urged investors from Britain and the Commonwealth to put their money into the Federation and assured them of the British Government's determination to back them if they did. Mr. Butler would not have said this, had he not believed it, and the only inference to be drawn is that, once more, somebody knew more about the government's intention than even he.

A few months after his speech he informed the House of Commons, and through the High Commissioner in Salisbury Sir Roy Welensky, that the British Government agreed to Nyasaland's withdrawal from the Federation. Sir Roy replied, from Salisbury, ". . . there is little if any honour left in dealing with the British Government. I say that Britain . . . is utterly reckless of the fate of the inhabitants of the present Federation".

In March 1963 the Federal Ministers were invited to London to see if at least the two Rhodesias could not be kept together in the Federation. The pattern of events repeated itself: Mr. Kaunda,

*During the Second War Mr. Sandys was a son-in-law of Mr. Churchill, whose words, "I have not become His Majesty's First Minister to preside over the disintegration of the British Empire" now echo faintly down the years.

already in virtual control in Northern Rhodesia, refused to attend the meeting unless his terms were accepted, and Mr. Butler told Sir Roy, "If we were free to decide, we would like to see the closest links between the Rhodesias . . . but we haven't any forces in Central Africa to impose our will".

Three days later came the end, when the Federal Ministers saw Mr. Butler again. "He looked wan and grey and ill", says Sir Roy, "averting his gaze he spoke rapidly and tonelessly". His message now was that *any* territory might secede, (ergo, Northern Rhodesia *and* Nyasaland).

Sir Roy asked Mr. Butler to inform Mr. Macmillan that he and his Ministers would not be able to lunch with the Prime Minister: "I don't want to be discourteous but I cannot accept the hospitality of a man who has betrayed me and my country". Mr. Butler "sat in silence, looking stricken", while messengers scurried away.

Sir Roy raised a last matter, that of the Barotse people in Northern Rhodesia, who wished to secede from Mr. Kaunda.* Mr. Butler, says Sir Roy, remained silent. "He seemed so near to collapse that I changed the subject."†

Such, in March 1963, was the end of the Federation, begun with such brave hope in 1953. This reduced the area of stability in Africa to a last bastion, composed of Southern Rhodesia, South Africa, and the two Portuguese territories. After that, the deluge.

All that remained was the formal liquidation of the Federation and the matter of Southern Rhodesia's independence. Independence had been thrust on the two lesser territories, both backward and unready for it. The logical next step was independence for Southern Rhodesia, far more advanced than the others, self-governing for forty years, raised by its own bootstraps to its status, without monetary or other help from others. More than thirty new "States" had been fabricated out of the tribal complex of Africa and were

---

*Among the Federal delegates was Mr. Lewanika, a son of King Lewanika of the Barotse, whose territory was guaranteed seventy years before by treaty negotiated with Queen Victoria. Mr. Lewanika asked Mr. Butler if Barotseland were to be allowed to secede from Northern Rhodesia: "the Barotse are not prepared to be ruled by Kaunda or any other African nationalist. My father, at his own request, made treaties with the British Government which you are now going to break". Followed a flurry of whispering among Mr. Butler's officials, but no answer was given. Sir Roy said, "Why can't you be honest with my Minister? Why can't he be told, so that he can tell the Litunga, that the Barotse have been sold down the river?"

†Mr. Macmillan and Mr. Butler both retired from political life soon after this, as Mr. Eden after Suez.

35

being propped up with British money while they clamoured for war in New York.* It was unimaginable, in 1963, that to Rhodesia alone, in all this continent, independence should be denied.

But this was the case, as the next eighteen months of doubletalk showed. Mr. Winston Field, Southern Rhodesian Prime Minister, now took up the burden. Looking back on Sir Roy Welensky's four thousand days, he resolved not to be washed away with waves of words. Firmly he informed Mr. Butler that his government would not attend the liquidation conference "unless we receive *in writing* from you an acceptable undertaking that Southern Rhodesia will receive its independence" concurrently with the secession of the two other territories.

Mr. Field felt that he had at last pinned the issue down. Mr. Butler's reply, smooth as silk, "accepted in principle" that Southern Rhodesia should "proceed through the normal processes to independence" and then stated "what we consider should be done" *before* independence could be granted. There should be many discussions on various matters before . . . and so on and so on.

Nothing *in writing*. The game of words went on.

Mr. Winston Field repeated his demand for an undertaking "in writing" and submitted that the record and achievements of Southern Rhodesia already constituted much more than "the normal processes to independence"; moreover, the other territories had been given independence without going through any such processes. This argument is unanswerable, but the London Government was not interested in arguments: it already knew the facts, and just wanted to keep Mr. Field stringing along.

Mr. Butler's reply was affable and as elusive as a soaped eel. Yes, indeed, he well knew Southern Rhodesia's proud record of achievement, and his Government repeated its acceptance, "in principle", that Southern Rhodesia should proceed "through the normal processes" and so on and so on. Above all, he said, Southern Rhodesia was still a member of the de facto defunct Federation, which could be brought to an end only by the passage of United

*In the five years 1960–1965 "Commonwealth" States in Africa received some £194,000,000 in grants, loans and technical assistance from Britain. At least three of these, Tanganyika, Zanzibar and Zambia, harbour the terrorist bands, trained in Moscow, Nanking and North Korea, which sporadically cross the Rhodesian border with instructions to "kill, burn, slash and maim", (vide Radio Zambia).

Kingdom legislation enacting that the Federation already destroyed in London should cease to exist and so on and so on.

(I imagine that the lawyers who draft these communications must writhe with mirth as they devise them. Sir Roy Welensky relates that he and his colleagues, after wrestling long with one such earlier message, tried to understand it by means of a diagram, and at last threw the diagram away in despair).

By now Mr. Winston Field, like Sir Roy before, was hopelessly befogged. His next letter no longer requested an undertaking "in writing" and asked only that Southern Rhodesia should receive independence "not later than the date when the dissolution of the Federation occurs". Apparently failing to perceive the trap, or still unwilling to believe in anything less than utter sincerity at the other end, he then invited Mr. Butler to discuss "the terms on which Southern Rhodesia would proceed to independence on the dissolution of the Federation".

Mr. Field was undone. Mr. Butler's legal advisers pounced on that phrase, "the terms", like eagles on a brood of chicks. But of course, of course, they replied (through Mr. Butler) more affably than ever, Southern Rhodesia should have its independence— "subject to the satisfactory conclusion of the discussions about *the terms*." (Mr. Kaunda's Northern Rhodesia and Dr. Banda's Nyasaland gained all they wanted without any palaver about "terms").

Thus the liquidation conference was held, in July 1963, and Mr. Winston Field and Mr. Ian Smith who accompanied him, came empty away. All that was determined was that the Federation, already dead, should formally expire in December 1963. Mr. Field and Mr. Smith were told privately that the matter of their independence would be finalized once the conference ended, but they had nothing "in writing", and when it was over found themselves in Southern Rhodesia, alone, and facing a sea of troubles, which, after two more years of doubletalk, Mr. Ian Smith and his government resolved to oppose and end.

Historically, the outstanding event of this ten-year story was the decline of the Conservative party in England, once a powerful element of stability in the world. The eclipse of its leaders was not brought about by advancing years but was the penalty of recurrent fiasco. Its headlong retreat from responsibility showed it to have lost the sense of purpose and national interest. It repeatedly ran

37

away from any loud clamour, whether from the Opposition benches or from the petty demagogues who hastened from Africa to London to exploit its weakness, and supported their demands by organized terrorism in the countries they left behind them. Its pretence that these represented "the people" was painful to watch, for it knew better. It offered the world the spectacle of a great government reacting like puppets on a string to the manipulation of any here-today-and-gone-tomorrow upstart who paraded himself in London as an "African nationalist". Above all, it set up a coterie of such in New York as a tribunal with authority to dictate the world's affairs.

If, as Mr. Sandys said, it has lost the will to govern, it has little claim to govern again, for it squandered the British heritage of faith-keeping and would command little confidence. If it cannot find in its ranks new men of another kind, who will stand for the British heritage (as Rhodesia stands today) its day may well be done.

The Socialist government which succeeded continued the method of doubletalk and out of that came at last what is colloquially known as Wilson's War. However, Mr. Wilson but continued in the Conservatives' ten-year footsteps. This was not a party matter, whatever else it might be. Some occult clutch seemed to drag both parties from fiasco to fiasco.

These fiascos led, in November 1965, to the Battle for Rhodesia.

THE CROSS AT KARIBA

The monument to the great Federation is the Kariba Dam, the symbol of what might have been and, if the Western governments returned to reason, what might yet be again. Power began to flow from it in 1960, when it was declared open by the Queen Mother, but the truth behind the splendid ceremonial of that day was that the Federation was already being destroyed thousands of miles away.

Thousands of Italian workmen built it in three years and a whole township of houses, schools, hospitals and roads sprang up on Kariba hill, in a country wild, peopled by primitive tribes, remote and previously inaccessible. Now the Italians are gone and when I was there, in 1966, the settlement was almost a ghost town, for petrol rationing kept away the throngs of visitors and fishermen from far away who otherwise would have reanimated it.

The Italians, nevertheless, left behind something greater than the dam: a token of man's indestructible hope and of the Christian's faith. They worked six-hour shifts, six-on-six-off, to beat the timetable, and succeeded, against great odds of flood and mishap. Some of them, and some African workmen, died of the heat, down there far below the Zambezi's bed. Yet the Italians, during their six-hour respite, built on the very top of the hill the loveliest church a man may see in many a day's march. They were craftsmen as well as artisans and adorned it as only men from Italy, perhaps, know how to adorn a church. It is circular and open to the air, because the congregation, then, was more than it could contain, and many knelt outside.

They dedicated it to the patron saint of workmen and to those who died during the toil: the names, Italian and tribal, are engraved on a common plate. They knew they would soon be gone and for the simple love of God built this exquisite place where they might worship while the work went on. The task, once done, was meant to uplift men on both sides of the great river, fertilize their lands and improve their lives: what better signature to it than the sign of the cross? On the church's roof they set a great cross, which boatmen on the lake made by the dam, if they lose their bearings, may see from forty miles away.

39

The waters stored by the dam rose to form the biggest man-made lake in the world: an inland sea it seemed when I flew over it. The spreading lake, too, brought new problems. The people who lived on the river's banks from time unknown, the Batonka (they with quills through their noses and front teeth removed) violently objected to this, the white man's disturbance of their solitude, but in time they were persuaded, moved away, and contentedly settled in new lands. Then came the game, big and small. The larger animals were able, with encouragement, to swim to land as the water rose, but the smaller ones had to be tenderly caught and saved. This rescue operation by means of rafts, boats, nets, nylon ropes and tranquilliser drugs was something new in the world, an epic, done by devoted men of the Game Department. Only the rhinoceros, among the big creatures, sometimes refused to shift, and their transport to dry land was an undertaking, unimaginable before it was achieved.

What followed was as darkness to light. Today, on both sides of the river, soldiers keep watch against each other, and from either side aeroplanes patrol to see what goes on. The great turbines have to be guarded by day and night. From the northern side Radio Zambia incites the tribesmen on the southern one to murder and arson. The Moscow- and Nanking-trained terrorists slip across the 400-mile border in the darkness, and in Rhodesia a handful of police and helicopters watch to stop them before they get too far with their Chinese and Russian bombs and weapons. But for the Western governments and their patronage of these "African nationalists", save the mark, all would now be as it was before. Law and order would reign and men on both sides of the river, black and white, would live in amity, sleep secure at night, and work unafraid by day.

On the hilltop the cross stands between the new severed territories. The church is not quite deserted, though its congregation is gone. The Italian priest has stayed: I was told that he would not leave because he believed he had much work to do among the Africans. Three nuns are there, too, and early each morning he celebrates Mass, alone with them.

I went to the church and on the steps met a lady with (I thought) a Northumberland accent, who looked at me and said, hesitantly, "I'm not a Catholic". "Shall we go in?" I said, and we went.

The three white nuns prayed and told their rosaries and presently the priest came in, with an African acolyte, and celebrated mass as the sun rose over Kariba.

The Mass, whatever your belief or unbelief, is a majestic ritual, worthy of a king of kings. In this setting, beneath the great cross and the blue African sky, with dogs of war waiting to be unleashed around and the distant world howling Havoc, I felt in it a particular meaning and poignancy.

Before we watch the Battle for Rhodesia itself, come with me, gentle reader, and look at the means by which matters were brought to that pass, by which the Western world was persuaded (or for some ulterior motive professed to be persuaded) that "African nationalists" spoke for "the people" of these parts and that the white man must be driven hence.

Imagine (but in your secure, watertight, all-electric, main-drained abode this will be hard), imagine a thatched, mud and wattle hut in the African bush, in the silent and unholy night. The desert itself is not much more lonely. The next kraal is a mile away, the nearest township twenty miles, help, in effect, a million miles. At the weekend thousands of young men have come from Salisbury, Bulawayo or another place, among them the town-tainted wastrels and neerdowells (all cities, white and black, produce quantities of these, as many British and American citizens well know today). Among these, again, are those few who have been trained in arson and murder, cattle-maiming and crop-destruction, in faraway Asia, and around them are a larger number who have not been so far but have listened to those others and caught the taint.

You, in your thatched hut in the black, lightless night, cannot read or write. Your world is bounded by the tribe and its tradition, which is just what memory has handed down from the remote recesses of time. Because you have no "history", as the West knows it, your memory is long and keen and vivid, and although you have always slept in peace your flesh still chills at the elders' tales of those other, million and one African nights, stretching back to the unknown beginning: the nights which were rent asunder by the sudden clamour of "Kill, kill" around the huts, the shrieks of the old men and women (the young tribesman might not marry before his assegai was blooded and this blood was cheapest) and the roar of flames. A few minutes and all was done. The captives were gone, to the slaver, and the bodies lay among the embers, which cast a fading glow into that black, black, friendless night.

Now these nights, suddenly and violently, have come again. The young men have been and gone, and before they left spread the word among the kraals: wreck the dips, poison the fodder, hamstring the cattle, stone the white man's car, slash his crops: do all this, or we will burn you when we come again.

So you lie and fear to sleep, in your lonely, thatched hut. Or perhaps you take your babes and creep away into the bush, to try and sleep in a cave or beneath a tree. If you stay in your hut, then at last you *do* sleep, deeply, immovably, unwakeably, as tribes-people sleep. You do not smell the burning bark-strips, even when the flames rise to the thatch, for the smoke goes upward, until with a sudden roar the roof falls on you.

This is original Africa, now, after seventy years of peace, being rekindled as ancient embers might be stirred. This is the African reality which Western politicians call "African nationalism", which newspapers, radio and television conceal from the mass-audience.

Next morning, if you live, you talk endlessly with the others around, and try to understand. Why are "our children" doing this? The only world you know ends at the headman's boundary, but you gather, without comprehending, that "the children" are being told in the outer world to do these things, that mysterious outer world where your protectors have lived from the time of the great Queen who first made your nights secure. What is this new thing? Why cannot the Chief protect you, or your white "fathers".

What would you do, gentle reader, if you were the Chief of 70,000 tribespeople in this district of some 120 miles by 30: or if you were the District Commissioner, with his six white and twelve black police? What would you do if you were in *their* place and you were told that the distant Protector would no longer protect you, because you do not speak for "the people"?

I went over the story of one such affair on the spot. It occurred during the eighteen months following the destruction of the Federation and was meant to force the hand of London into capitulation in Southern Rhodesia, as it had been forced by the same means in Northern Rhodesia and Nyasaland. The word had gone round: the white man is weak: strike, strike!

This particular reign of terror (other districts suffered similarly) was brought under control in two days, by the arrival of a small force of black troops and the use of a few helicopters. The eyes watching from above unnerved the terrorists and reassured the tribesfolk, who slowly returned to their huts to sleep after spending cold nights, men, women and children, in the bush. Freed from the terror, they

43

began to report the presence of any "intimidator" who showed himself. Today the district is a picture of peace, where the people work and sleep without fear, the cattle thrive, dipping goes on as authority insists. Any who go there may see a tribe happy in its fashion.

These are the facts of what happens. The other fact is that such deeds of criminal violence are presented to the Western world by its newspapers, radio and television as the gallant exploits of "freedom fighters", "guerillas" and "outlawed African nationalists". This constantly happens, and has happened again as I write; the burning and killing of black folk by black folk are presented as an understandable reaction against the white man's authority.

Let me show you, good reader, what truly occurs. These men are picked up somehwere in Rhodesia and smuggled over the border to Lusaka in Zambia, where are the terrorist headquarters. They seem to be studied there and after a few weeks are forwarded by road to Dar es Salaam in Tanganyika, which today seems to be a Communist outpost, or colony, on the north-eastern coast of Africa. From there they go by air to Moscow, Nanking or North Korea, are trained in the use of weapons, explosives and petrol for some months, and then return by the same route to Dar es Salaam, Lusaka and Rhodesia.

I have seen the statements made by many of these men, who were captured, and they all tell the same story, save for the few who refuse to say anything at all. The others describe their experiences similarly and in detail and by cross-checking one can see that they are true. They are all provided with a "cover story" for use if captured, and it is always the same story: that they were induced to go to Moscow (or Peking, or North Korea) by the offer of "a scholarship" which would qualify them for a better post on their return to Rhodesia: they say they would not have gone if they had known the real purpose; but they all agree that, when they discovered it, they submitted without ado to the training in weapons, explosives and the rest. Some of them have been caught with caches of Russian- and Chinese-marked weapons and bombs.

The communist budget for this Operation Africa must be enormous. The permanent shuttle-service by air between Dar es Salaam and the terrorist training-centres in Moscow, Nanking and North Korea alone must be most costly. During their stay there, and in Dar es Salaam and Lusaka, they have to be housed, fed, clothed and given money. A large staff in the Russian and Chinese embassies at Dar es Salaam is needed to supervise their reception and transport, and this in addition to the cost of all the instructors and buildings at the other end.

When British politicians in London and American ones in Washington and at the United Nations in New York insist that a solution "acceptable to the African people" must be attained in Rhodesia, they mean *these* people, for they refuse to listen to their victims, the tribespeople, their headman and chiefs, who are the true "people". The arrogant and ignorant disdain shown by politicians from England, particularly, towards them during the last five years has been a spectacle, as humiliating to responsible white folk as was Mr. Chamberlain's performance at Munich and President Roosevelt's at Yalta. Every day now the question poses itself larger and ever larger: why is America, and Britain under America's wing, supporting communism in Africa? Why are they fulfilling Lenin's plan?

But for that, peace would return to Africa. The terrorist gangs were brought under firm control, without great difficulty, in the year preceding UDI, and but for the organization in the communist East and the support it receives from "the free world" in the West, they would never be heard of again. In fact, very much will be heard of them during the rest of 1966 and in 1967 if general war has by then not occurred, because this is considered to be the now-or-never time for the complete subjugation of Africa. The greatest possible amount of violence will for this reason be unloosed in order that The Voice of America (today, apparently a Mr. Goldberg) may declare that this is The Voice of Africa speaking.*

From the support of terrorism in Southern Africa to war is but a short step. Such a war, obviously, would not be one "against Communism", but, in truth, in support of it, because the impulse comes from that quarter, and the encouragement from the professedly opposite one.

This is the time set for that war, and if the world somehow skids

---

*In May 1966 Mr. Goldberg announced that the United States was determined to see that Mr. Ian Smith did not succeed and that the principle of "majority rule" must prevail in Rhodesia the reader has seen that in London and Washington the reign of terror instigated from Moscow and Nanking is always represented as the expression of "the majority".

45

past the peril in coming months it will be blessed indeed. As by careful planning, all the sources of war conjoin at this moment in time: the case against South Africa at the International Court, the published plan for war on South Africa (see a later chapter), the siege of Rhodesia, the communist terrorism in Rhodesia, the war-mongering majority of irresponsibles in the United Nations, and, above all, the now public incitement by the United States (if its representative there speaks for the President, as one must assume, and not against him).

A perilous brink, my masters, and I trust that you may think on these things when next you hear or read about "freedom fighters" or "guerillas" in Rhodesia. May your minds then conjure up the image of that constant shuttle-service between Lusaka, Dar es Salaam and the distant communist terrorist-camps; of the encouragement given to all that by your politicians in London, Washington and New York; and of that lonely mud-and-wattle hut blazing in the night with black folk trapped inside.

Let us go back for a moment to that place. Near the charred site of such a hut I talked with the Chief, in his good suit, white helmet, and chief's badge. A German film-cameraman, in search of the picturesque, once asked the District Commissioner here if he would ask the Chief to pose "in his ostrich feathers". This one, who has been half round the world twice, had none and if he ever saw an ostrich feather, then perhaps in Bond Street or Fifth Avenue. The only tribal costume ever known in this tribe was nothing, and to-day's tribesman there has long worn white man's clothing.

I sat beside him in his little court while he adjudged what I thought must be a small matter, for he tried it in a room and few came to listen, whereas for anything of tribal importance the people would have gathered in thousands around the big indaba tree outside. Thus I was surprised when he murmured to me the dread word, "Arson", for I knew the terrorists were gone.

Benign and judicial as any High Court judge in the West, he questioned the complainant (a woman) and I learned, as he translated for me, that the matter was but a domestic one. "I want to know," said she, "why my husband burned my hut". The Chief looked at the husband: "Well", he said, penitently, "I came home from a beerdrink and went to her hut" (she was his second wife) "but she called out 'I am tired'." Such words are not unkown in

46

the West, I am told, but the husband did not put the proverbial Western counter-question. He was a tribesman and knew a woman's place. He demanded to know what she had been doing, that she was tired, whereon she admitted him. But his question, repeated, remained unanswered, so that he removed the children and whatever else the hut contained and burned it (an act, I believe, of symbolic meaning). The Chief quietly interrupted his eloquence (the tribesman, if allowed, will talk forever) and asked, "Do you love your wife?", and the husband said, Yes, but he was very, very drunk that night. Thus the Chief sorted the thing out, in a few moments, to its happy ending, and as we left the tribesfolk outside made respectful farewell, hands clapping in unison and a shrill, birdlike call.

These, fellow seekers after knowledge, are "the African people". Given the protection, against other tribes (today, against the outer world) which they have had for seventy years, they know how to manage their affairs and live in content. This Chief, and nearly all the people I met, black and white, spoke bitterly of the earlier terror by night, applauded what had been done to end it, and prayed only that it might never return. Word had reached them of what went on in neighbouring, now "independent" territories and their fear, outweighing every other thought, was that the old times of killing and burning should come again.

I asked the Chief if he had spoken for independence at the great Indaba of over six hundred chiefs before UDI Yes, he said, they had discussed and debated for five days, every man his say, and every one agreed that, as the protector no longer protected and was weak, they must "cut the strings" and look for protection to their own government.

Was all well now, I asked. Yes, he said, very well: the people no longer went in fear, they could sleep and tend their cattle and work their fields in peace. He had been to London, been turned away, and could not comprehend why the great men there listened to "our children" (the terrorists) and ignored the leaders of the people. I recalled a day, just before Independence, when a British Prime Minister (after one week in Rhodesia and meeting forty-six people) said in the Commons, "The Chiefs cannot, by the widest stretch of imagination, be said to be capable of representing the African population as a whole".

A lot of ignorance is a dangerous thing. Unless and until the tribal system can be destroyed (and it goes back beyond any time that we can record) they and only they are so capable, and a man who thus frivols with the basic fact of African life is as a child who plays around a gusher with a firecracker.

"What do you think of one-man-one-vote?" I said. To the ordinary tribesman even the question would be incomprehensible. The Chief was a travelled man and knew what was meant. These people, from chief to kraalsman, always choose words which will not offend, and, fearing to affront, he said deprecatingly, "I think that is not good here. This country must grow", he made a gesture towards a tall tree, "like that". "Is there anything you need here?", I asked. "Yes", he said, "more big schools" (he meant secondary schools: two days later, as it happened, the Government announced a new African education programme providing for three hundred new secondary schools in the next ten years).

As I came away I thought of smoking ruins, of wrecked dips, dead cattle, hamstrung beasts unable to rise, of a lonely white farmer or two gunned down through an open window. All that was done, and could not come again unless it came from outside. But the voices from across the border, from London, from something incomprehensible to "the African people" called the United Nations in New York continued their incitement: the shuttle-service between Dar es Salaam and communist Asia plied on . . .

The terror by night still lurked in the alien shadows.

Picture the burning hut to yourself, gentle and listless reader, for with your tacit assent and that of your Members and Congressmen these things are done.

During the two years that followed the break-up of the Federation the alien-organized terrorism continued in the kraals and the chiefs clamoured for the help which their government could not give, because of the obsession, or pretence, in London that the terrorists "represented the people".

In June–July of 1964 Mr. Ian Smith arranged for twenty-nine senior chiefs to visit many countries of the strange, new world. They were received with ceremony by the Pope in Rome and by Ministers in India, but the British Prime Minister refused to see them and they achieved only two half-hours with Mr. Duncan Sandys, who told them that in London's opinion the "African nationalists" had the following of the people. The chiefs pointed out that whatever following these had came out of intimidation by murder and arson. Mr. Sandys intimated that methods did not concern him, he was satisfied that they *had* the following. Thereon the chiefs said they were law-abiding people but by calling out their impis they could soon show who were the true leaders.

Mr. Sandys at once retreated, with the familiar cry of "no violence": on all these occasions the chiefs were told that "a following" produced by violence had been "demonstrated" but that they must not demonstrate a following by replying to violence with counter-violence.

The chiefs returned to Rhodesia humiliated and angry and, after taking counsel with all the other chiefs and headmen, told Mr. Ian Smith of their strong support for independence, the only way in which peace and law could return to the kraals. Mr. Smith went to London, for some more doubletalk, and was told that Southern Rhodesia could only receive independence if the British Government were given "evidence" and "views freely expressed by the population" that the majority supported him. (During seven weeks of this period 1,725 acts of terrorism, from murder down to cattle-maiming, were committed, the two "African nationalist" parties were banned, and the kraals became peaceful again).

Mr. Smith, still hoping to satisfy London, then set about to "ascertain opinion" in the only possible way, in Africa, by consulting the chiefs and headmen, some seven hundred of whom gathered at

Domboshawa in October 1964 and for five days reasoned together in the traditional tribal way.

Each in turn rose at the end and called for "the strings" to be cut, that is, the bond with England severed, and independence be given. They were embittered by the indignity of their leaders' reception in London, by the refusal to see, listen to or learn the truth, and by the deference shown there to the organizers of terror. Some of their words deserve record:

"It is amazing that anyone who lives six thousand miles away should think they understand conditions here."

"We have asked the British Prime Minister to come here and confront us . . . The thing that depresses us is that his representative is here next door in Northern Rhodesia and has not the courtesy to come . . . You see for yourselves the manners of a person who lives six thousand miles away."

"There is no such thing as one man, one vote, casting your vote on a piece of paper. This is quite foreign to our way of life. By our customs, our method of voting is to discuss the matter openly, as we are doing today in this hall. After a matter has been fully discussed anyone who has any objection is invited to stand up and give his reasons for objecting. This is our traditional method of reaching unanimity . . . We have seen that Britain does not wish to respect our customs, she is destroying them."

"I am one of those who visited Britain. Face to face they said to us, they no longer recognize the chiefs, they only recognize two people who are our children, Joshua Nkomo and Ndabaningi Sithole" (the leaders of the two banned parties which were identified with the reign of terror).

"Right from the beginning we were recognized as the leaders of the people, by the missionaries to whom the chiefs in council first gave land: by Rhodes and by Queen Victoria when he sent Chief Lotsha to her as his representative: in 1914 and again in 1939 it was we chiefs who called our people to the aid of Britain. The King, with his Queen and their two daughters, came especially to thank the chiefs for that. When the Queen Mother came here I, together with all the chiefs, presented her with our token of loyalty . . . Now I wonder if the London we have always known still exists. This is perhaps another London which has emerged because they suddenly cannot remember all that the chiefs have done . . . It makes us believe that it is the British Government that is saying to these young thugs, 'Go and kill your fathers'. In London they know about the deeds of these young thugs yet they have not bestirred themselves nor yet even raised a voice in protest. This convinces me that they are the ones who are behind it all . . ."

"Where Rhodes met the chiefs in the Matopos there was an enormous boulder high up above them on the hill. Recently that boulder tumbled down to the bottom. This is a sign that we who are gathered here must come to a decision . . . When that rock fell it indicated to us to cut the strings and have our independence so that we can live our own life in this our land."

You observe, companion of these pages, that these people, who do not write down their history, carry living history in them. Everything that has gone before is there, in its proper place and given its rightful meaning. And by their "traditional method of reaching unanimity" they reach truth. Consider those words, "This convinces me that they are the ones that are behind it all". They recall the child's cry at the court of the unclothed king: "The king is naked". What folk in the enlightened West fear to say, these people discern and utter.

Consider also that fallen boulder. A hundred years from now that event will be part of their living, though unwritten history, in its right place and given its apt significance: "The protector is gone: we must cut the strings".

1965 began and the doubletalk continued: "every time we moved nearer to them, they moved away", said Mr. Ian Smith later. In February, at last, a British Minister agreed to meet the chiefs in another great indaba at Domboshawa. The kopje at Domboshawa has an especial place in the beliefs and customs of the local tribes. They believe it to be the haunt of spirits, and not of benign ones, apparently, because when the Queen Mother was there tribesmen were posted round about with guns, which they fired to keep the spirits away. This did not happen when Mr. Arthur Bottomley, Commonwealth Secretary, arrived; possibly one may attribute the unhappy outcome to the hostile spirits.

I have contemplated political gentlemen for nearly forty years and cannot recall one who seemed less suitable for the post he filled. Hailing from Walthamstow, he seems to have risen in politics through the Labour Party machine, and knew nothing of Africa

51

(he once confused Zambia with Gambia). He was a natural master of the *mot injuste* and aroused in others that unease which the sight of a hippopotamus walking on eggs would cause. His mind moved in a world of ballots, shows of hands, card votes, motions and amendments, points of order and rulings from the chair, and he tried hard to ascertain that the chiefs had consulted their people by such methods: when this baffled them, he thought they were evading his interrogation.

Some of the chiefs remembered Rhodes and Lobengula and even the four Household Cavalry officers sent by Queen Victoria* to impress that king. When they contemplated Mr. Bottomley they felt that the boulder's fall was significant indeed.

Mr. Bottomley, facing the red-robed figures, courteously instructed them that there were "some differences of opinion among the African peoples": however, he would listen to their views. His advisers were also maladroit, for someone put into his mouth two native proverbs, "A river is filled by its tributaries" and "The breast of man is a granary". The use of tribal idiom is perilous, unless you have some acquaintance with the allusive and indirect form of speech used by tribesmen, and Mr. Bottomley asked for one Chief's comment, that a little knowledge is a dangerous thing.

The Chiefs spoke in Sindebele or Shona yet their tongue was nearer to that which Shakespeare spake than the man from Whitehall's. Their theme was always the same: protest against the present Britain, and reminder of the British past:

"You know full well that many people have died, have been incinerated in their huts, that our huts are thatched with grass. It seems clear that the British Government has no concern for us. You said we have proverbs that say this and that: to my mind it would have become you better to come here humbly to learn from us Chiefs what the position is in this country. I stand here in fear because my home may be burning . . . You do not realize that we do not sleep of nights because of this fear that by the morning we and our children may be dead . . ."

"I am astounded to hear that the Chiefs and headmen are not

*They wore full regimentals, plumed helmets and shining cuirasses, thigh-high, bespurred boots and white buckskin breeches, scarlet coats and aiguelettes, golden swordbelts and tassels and the rest and were kept waiting a fortnight by Lobengula, who when at last he saw them asked only if the cuirasses would keep out bullets.

the leaders of the people. What have you been doing for seventy years that you have not discovered this before?"

"We waited here for you a whole week in October and then heard you were gone back to England . . . You, sir, if you had a thatched roof and your wife and children were incinerated in it, would you be content? Many of the Chiefs and Headmen here present have had their wives and children killed."

"A person from the British Government came through these parts and said there would be a wind of change and because of what the British Government then did the whole of Africa is now in turmoil and strife . . . Everywhere the people are fighting like dogs over a bone because the power was let fall into wrong hands . . . We live in fear because the Europeans overseas are giving our youngsters bombs and weapons . . . When we went to London . . . the British Ministers ran away and hid. One of them said, 'I can see you for thirty minutes' and then had the nerve to tell us, 'You are not the leaders of the people, Nkomo is the leader'."

"I stand so that you can see me, your servant who has had his houses burned and children and wives killed."

Then the repeated reminders of the past, with its pledges and protection given. Ever and again these men retold the story of peace that began with the meeting between Rhodes and Lobengula, the period that began with the Separator of the Fighting Bulls and now ended with the crashing boulder. That meeting in the Matopos was a monument, erected in their minds, which was more real to them than any marble statue to a white man:

"Rhodes set us our great example when he said that everybody must work together, put down their weapons and work as one community, and we did this and have lived very happily together. Had we known that this would be changed, we certainly would not have laid aside our weapons."

"From the time when I was a child, brought up by my fathers, the old people, they always made me understand that the British word and the British sense of justice was something that one had to look up to and therefore I have grown up to be what I am today . . . Now we have doubts whether England is still England, or whether she is standing on one side with some ulterior motive, and we are left with the impression that those who hold the reins in England are no longer British, probably some other nationality. And I say

53

this because I am certain that the British in the past would never have allowed this state of affairs to continue."

The reader will see that these men, though they spoke their own tongue, spoke with what was once the voice of England. Today one may borrow the words of a song and ask, Where are all the flowers gone? These eloquent words appeared to fall from Mr. Bottomley as water from feathers, and the next encounter (a week later he met the Council of Chiefs, twenty-six senior Chiefs elected by the rest) was still unhappier.

Mr. Bottomley began by informing the Council that he had seen the "African nationalist leaders", and my readers may care to put themselves inside the skin of the men who heard that, with their minds full of pictures of burning huts and death. He then asked the Chiefs to "demonstrate that they represent the bulk of African opinion", and informed them that they used "the ballot" in the election of traditional chiefs within the tribes. Even for Mr. Bottomley, this was an astounding assertion: chiefs are chiefs by tradition of birth.

One Chief, stung beyond endurance, said, "It is obvious to us, Sir, that however much truth we speak it is not the intention of our honoured guest to be satisfied with what we know to be the truth. If we take him to the grave of people killed, to the graves of children murdered, to wrecked churches and schools and diptanks, he still would not be satisfied that this was done by the African nationalists. If I had my way, I would say, 'Let us get out of this meeting. Let Mr. Bottomley hand over government to these people and see what would happen . . .'"

Any meeting of minds between Mr. Bottomley and these men was impossible. To them, Mr. Bottomley was a hostile and incomprehensible figure: to him, they were slippery customers who would not stand up to questions about "ballots" and "votes". From first to last Mr. Bottomley ignored every reference to what was the very root of the matter: the terror in the kraals. At the end, when one chief personally asked him, "What *do* you want? If you want us to demonstrate our following, let us call out our impis and restore law and order", Mr. Bottomley patted his shoulder and said something which sounded like, "Oh, Oi pray yew, no violence".

The meeting had to be wound up, when its hopelessness became clear, by a man of different kind, young, able, active, airman, farmer, now Minister: Mr. William Harper, of Internal Affairs. He spoke language which both parties could understand, saying (for the benefit of Mr. Bottomley) that they were on "completely different wavelengths", and (for that of the Chiefs) that "the hippo and the lion do not talk the same language". Possibly in a last, faint hope of reaching Mr. Bottomley's mind, he explained that the tribal system and the Western electoral system were as worlds apart, and that the best evidence of the hold of the tribal system on "the people" was that those who sought political power in the land had to resort to force to try and upset it.

With that Mr. Bottomley went his way, having learned and forgotten nothing, 1965 wore on, and the course of human events neared the point where Rhodesia would be driven to declare independence, if only to be able to put down the terror and settle the land again. At the last instant (in October) Mr. Harold Wilson consented to meet the Council of Chiefs (for ninety minutes). He refused to have the proceedings recorded so that no verbatim exists (a fortnight later Mr. Wilson tape-recorded and published a telephone conversation with Mr. Ian Smith, without informing Mr. Smith).

From notes made by the Chiefs (who protested against the refusal to have the meeting recorded) it is clear that they spoke as they had spoken to Mr. Bottomley: that is, they recalled the British past, pointed to the terror in the kraals and to the "African nationalists" as its organizers, and said they wanted independence so that they could handle it, as the British Government encouraged it.

Like Mr. Bottomley, Mr. Wilson, when he reported to the Commons, ignored the great issue, the terror. He disparaged the Chiefs as being "paid by the Rhodesian Government". They do receive up to a maximum of about £550 in salary and allowances. British M.P.'s get £1,750 and have been heard to ask for more.

Finally, Mr. Wilson fired his memorable dictum, based on a non-recorded meeting of ninety minutes, that the Chiefs were not capable, "by the widest stretch of imagination", of representing the African population as a whole. This stupendous misjudgment cleared the way for another period of "African nationalist" courtship in London, and produced an impasse in the Rhodesian negotiations which could only be broken by "cutting the strings" and declaring Independence.

The descents on Africa during these twelve years of British Ministers, Conservative and Socialist, and their performances there, made people who live in Africa writhe with embarrassment: they were as some quite new form of human life. The same sensation was experienced earlier by those who lived in Europe, for instance, at the time when Mr. Chamberlain spoke of "plucking this flower safety from this nettle danger" by abandoning "a little country far away" to Hitler's invasion.

Six months later, when "sanctions" were in top gear and "talks" between London and Salisbury were arranged, in hope of a settlement, President Kaunda of Zambia renewed his clamour for Britain to attack Rhodesia. The London government, the newspapers then announced, assured him that "the rights of Rhodesia's four million Africans will be fully protected".

And the rights of *Zambia's* Africans? Zambia's independence was ushered in by the massacre of the Lumpa sect. They were Africans. Nobody in England cared or remonstrated. The "rights of four million Africans in Rhodesia", if London had its way, would obviously be "protected" in the same measure.

Their only true hope of protection lay in independence, and it was given them.

A few paragraphs back, alluding to Mr. Wilson's revelation to the House of Commons, which he made in tones of horror, that the Rhodesian Chiefs were "paid by the Rhodesian Government", I said that they received up to £550 in salary and allowances, whereas British M.P.'s get £1,750. I took this information from an authentic, but apparently outdated source, and a Member of the House of Commons corrects me. "British M.P.'s now get £3,250," he says. I am happy to be able to give the full truth of this matter, as it stands at the moment (I believe complaints have been heard in some quarters of the House that this £3,250 is inadequate and ought to be increased).

MISS PHOMBEYA'S TOE

The propagation of falsehood about Rhodesia by newspapers, radio and television has chiefly brought about the present "ridiculous situation" (Mr. Ian Smith) between Rhodesia and the mesmerized masses of the outer world, and in a later chapter I shall seek to persuade you, good people, of the means by which people are persuaded of that which is not true. I pause here to give a classic illustration of the method, hoping that you, percipient reader, will bear it in mind when in future you read, listen or look. It is the case of Miss Phombeya's toe which, with a little more forethought and planning, might have caused a big war.

For great wars may from small beginnings grow, and as Captain Jenkins's ear caused one between England and Spain (which enlarged into the greater war of the Austrian Succession) what might not Miss Phombeya's toe have effected, efficiently handled by the machines of mass-information? True, Captain Jenkins, de-eared by a Spanish coastguard, was left earless for eight years before the Commons heard his tale (did he say, "Those who have ears to hear . . .?) and rose in fury against Spain. Possibly a bellicose reason was desired in 1739 which was not sought in 1731: "history" does not say.

Then again, the goods and chattels of Don Pacifico, a Portuguese Jew, nearly caused a war, for he was by chance of birth in Gibraltar a British subject, so that Lord Palmerston sent the British fleet to Greece to obtain redress for that act of pillage in Athens.

Therefore the world may have been fortunate in being spared grave consequences arising from Miss Phombeya's toe.

Miss Phombeya, a Malawi girl of twenty was one of a "Number of Ladies Present at the Scene" (Mr. Justice Southworth uses the public-convenience labels throughout his report and one hears a chuckle coming from the chambers where he prepared it) when Mr. Macmillan arrived at Blantyre in Nyasaland (now Malawi) in January 1960. He had just announced "the wind of change" at Lagos; this, being reported everywhere as an intimation that Nyasaland would be allowed to break up the Federation, encouraged the Malawi Congress Party to arrange a nice little demonstration for him at Blantyre, to reinforce his faith in the desire of "the

57

African people" for independence now, now, now. The representatives of *The Times*, the *News-Chronicle*, the *Standard* and the whole of the daily press also were there.

The reports which reached London that evening, and from there the world, variously estimated "the Number of Ladies and Gentlemen Present at the Scene" at two hundred up to two thousand. They spoke of "shaming scenes" and "a sickening spectacle" provoked by "the stupidity of the Nyasaland white police officers" and "an ugly situation" provoked by "a few young undisciplined policemen" who "stamped with heavy boots on bare feet" and went "berserk" and were "frenzied", of "baton-swinging", of "hysterical white settlers", of "Africans being seized indiscriminately" and "bundled roughly with punches and whip slashes into caged lorries", of other Africans being "grabbed and hurled, yelling and struggling" into a jeep, of Black Marias, and much more.

Through all this Mr. Macmillan, in Ryall's Hotel, quietly ate his pheasant especially flown from Scotland (one report changed this to "grouse", as being more suitable fare for a Scotsman: another added local colour to the tumultuous scene by putting in some non-existent "eucalyptus trees").

By that evening the "build-up" of the story had begun and one of the white police inspectors engaged remarked to his wife, as he listened to the B.B.C.'s depictment of what had occurred, "They must have gone to another incident than the one I went to". An African merchant who also heard it also was "surprised when I heard there was a rioting and beating, and so on . . . because there was no such thing at all". An American missionary of twenty-three years residence in Malawi, Mr. Barr, said when he heard the incident described as "a riot", "Riot. What riot?"

No matter: the build-up went on in the manner familiar to those who know the news-rooms of British and American newspapers. By the time it reached the Swedish *Stockholms Tidningen*, it took this shape, in shrieking headlines: "THE AGGRESSION OF THE WHITE POLICE FRIGHTENS THE BRITISH", and the report of the "violent riot" continued:

"The black masses acted calmly and with restraint until white police started to tear their banners away and attacked them with their truncheons. With uncontrolled brutality they whipped the black women and men and received willing assistance from local white civilians. The incident was also immediately echoed in the English Parliament where the Minister for Colonial Affairs promised the indignant home front to undertake at once an official investigation . . . the incident has opened the eyes of the English public to the Police State conditions which prevail in Rhodesia and Nyasaland . . . aggressions by the whites . . . something has to be done to curb the white extremists . . ."

In ever-growing form these reports spread over the world, until, two days later the *Daily Herald* in big headlines demanded, NAME THESE GUILTY MEN! STOP THESE BULLIES ONCE AND FOR ALL! It went on to speak of "a shameful, brutal, UNNECESSARY clash between police and African demonstrators, provoked by senior British police officers". What happened could not be denied, it said, because it took place "under the eyes of experienced reporters". NAME (it cried) the plain clothes officer who, in a state of frenzy . . . started the whole thing. NAME the senior officer who started lashing out with his baton. NAME the officer in charge of the whole operation. This brutal, barbarous, bullying attitude of mind must be kicked out of the colonial administration. No wonder that "hatred boils up in the hearts of friendly coloured folk when boneheads are let loose to knock them around with batons. NAME the men . . . PROSECUTE them."

By this time the affair was an international headline one. Questions In The House had been asked, and the thought of such gives Ministers nightmares.* The Minister yielded, fortunately as it transpired. Mr. Justice Southworth of the Nyasaland High Court was appointed to investigate the matter. He is evidently a man of subtle humour, as well as judicial impartiality, and his report greatly adds to the gaiety of nations, if any of that commodity remains. I recommend any who enjoy a good laugh to read it, even if they have to go to the British Museum for it.

At enormous expense the enquiry was held. It lasted four weeks and two days. Eighty-one witnesses were heard, including ten news-

---

*A literary curiosity: Mr. Nicholas Monsarrat's novel *The Tribe That Lost Its Head*, published several years earlier, gives an exact picture, in fictional form, of such an incident, progressively swollen by newspapers until all resemblance to the original happening is lost; in the imaginary case presented by him the same pattern is followed, leading through Questions In The House to the involvement of the government, and to a climax of killing and rapine. Fortunately, the case of Miss Phombeya's toe came to a ludicrous end, but the denouement might have been much graver.

paper correspondents who were invited to substantiate what they reported (although the day was cool when he was examined, one of them perspired so much that he appeared to be wearing drop earrings, a friend tells me). Six counsel were engaged, including the Nyasaland Solicitor General. The report covers 125 pages and its author's grave portraiture of The Ladies and Gentlemen in the witness-box deserves publication in paperback form throughout the English-speaking world.

It deflates the newsroom-inflated balloon to the size of a shrivelled pea. The brutal white police were thirteen in number, and one plainclothes one who took photographs (fortunately, because many of these showed what in truth occurred). They wore light walking shoes (not "heavy boots") and seven of them carried swagger-sticks weighing four and a quarter ounces (not "batons" or "truncheons" or "whips"). Some of them were former "London Bobbies" or from other British police forces (some of the reports said there would have been no trouble if only "London Bobbies" had handled the affair). They rapped and prodded unruly demonstrators with these swagger sticks to get them back on the sidelines.

The crowd, Mr. Justice Southworth estimates on the strength of all the evidence, was between eight hundred and a thousand people (not 2,000), nearly all of them onlookers, come only to look. The actual demonstrators numbered between fifty and eighty, but he thinks fifty nearer. The police had a landrover and a Bedford truck, the truck covered with wiremesh against stone-throwing, (not "Black Marias" or "caged lorries"). Thirty-five demonstrators were removed, but not "hurled" or "bundled" into these vehicles: they fought to get in, to the perplexity of the reporters present, who do not know that "Get arrested" is an instruction given on these occasions.

The actual demonstrators were a small group who broke out of the cordon into the road. These were headed by five Young Ladies, of whom Miss Phombeya was the most active, the prima ballerina, as it were. The behaviour of these Young Ladies, again, appeared to the newspapermen, unfamiliar with the African scene, to indicate irrepressible emotion and enthusiasm for some cause, for they shouted and danced themselves into a frenzy (one of the young men around them threw himself into a mud-puddle, tore off his coat and threw it at the police). Those who live in Africa know that

60

dancing is the native form of self-expression among the tribal peoples, and often ends in an eye-rolling condition where the dancer throws himself or herself or falls to the ground. Miss Phombeya and her friends were in fact dancing (and between you and me, friend reader, if ever you are in my part of the world I can show you something of this kind any Sunday you choose).

They continued to self-express themselves in this manner in the truck which took them away. Mr. Barr, the American missionary, says "The girls and several of the boys were carrying on their dancing rhythm similar to a normal village dance, inside the van". Mrs. Warr, a white lady, also describes one of the Young Ladies in the truck "giving us all a little dance, clapping her hands and seeming quite happy".

In the course of the little melée someone trod on Miss Phombeya's toe. Perhaps then, or perhaps at the climactic moment of her dance, she fell to the ground, and was courteously helped to her feet by a police inspector. A photograph of this episode was published in London and over the world as "Police slap down girl demonstrator".

Says Mr. Justice Southworth, "In the course of the disturbance, two or three of the demonstrators kicked or struck European police officers, and three European police officers kicked or struck demonstrators. One young lady had her foot trodden on by a police officer, and sustained a slight injury. The two officers who kicked demonstrators say they did this to make the demonstrators let go of them when they were dragged into the crowd: and the officer who trod on the lady's foot has explained how this was done by accident, an explanation which on the evidence one would not be entitled to reject. One other young lady may or may not have had her foot trodden on on this occasion, but if this occurred, it appears to have been done accidentally by someone in the crowd. The distance between the two furthest points between which the demonstrators moved throughout the course of the demonstration is about eighty yards. The entire incident took place on a straight stretch of road covering an area less than one-sixth the size of a football field . . . and appears to have occupied not more than forty minutes".

Mr. Justice Southworth's concluding sentences may have given him as much pleasure as they give today's reader. They place his report high among the literature of humour. More than that, if this standard of reporting were kept by newspapers, radio and television, peace in Africa, and in the world, would be secure:

"As far as can be ascertained the amount of skin lost by both police and demonstrators as a result of injuries received on this occasion would hardly cover an area of one square inch, probably no more than the area of a penny postage stamp: and it does not appear that the amount of blood that was shed would be sufficient to test the capacity of an ordinary mustard spoon. Contemplating the measure of the injuries sustained by the demonstrators, one cannot avoid the reflection that when the face of Helen launched a thousand ships, and brought Agamemnon and the great Achilles to the shores of Phrygia, it hardly achieved as much as Miss Phombeya's toe when it brought the paladins of Fleet Street in the aerial argosies of our day across two continents to appear before your Commissioner in the remote highlands of middle Africa."

May you bear those words in mind, reader of mine, when next you read or hear such tales of mystery and imagination as those which I have quoted earlier in this chapter.

And may I, in the role of old Polonius, lay one more precept in your memory. The tale of Miss Phombeya's toe, which reached you in such inflammatory form, might be said at least to have been founded in fact. Miss Phombeya *had* a toe, probably ten, and one was trodden. Even such a grain of truth, the size of a mustard seed, is not to be found in many reports published or depicted about Southern Africa today. I have a collection of a score or more of such reports, completely invented, and will enumerate some of them later.

I think you never heard one word about the massacre of 480 people, black, white and brown, men, women and babes, in Angola in March 1961. You heard a great deal, as you have now seen, about Miss Phombeya's toe in January 1960.

INDEPENDENCE

November The Eleventh, and famous words (slightly changed) coming over the air: "Whereas in the course of human affairs . . ."

I foresaw this five years earlier and then made plans to go to Rhodesia and follow events, but was hindered. I had long stopped writing: now the phrases, "The first western nation in two decades to say 'So far and no further' . . . and "A role of worldwide significance" jolted me into the resolve to fare once more unto the breach.

Particularly the words, "a role of worldwide significance". This pricked my interest like a spur. Nowadays, among governments, truth hid its head: there was only cant about "world peace" and "the United Nations" while the body so-called obviously was devised as the instrument of new war. These words of Mr. Ian Smith and the men around him seemed to mean that they saw the whole shape of the great Plan to obliterate nations in a world state and, like the Chiefs at Domboshawa, were not afraid to say "The king is naked". They wanted independence, in truth, from this scheme and only from Britain because of Britain's part in it. They realized that Rhodesia was the linchpin in the remaining area of peace and stability in Africa, and if it were knocked out, the way would be clear for the final move in the great game. I wondered that men so far from the hub of international machinations should see so clearly what all others, at the naked king's court, professed not to perceive. When I came to know these men, later, I was equally surprised by their clear understanding of what was in truth at stake and by their determination to hold the pass.

November The Eleventh! As I heard the words, somewhere in South Africa, I saw myself lean against the wall of a Flanders farmhouse in the drizzling dusk and watch the horse-gunners riding to their lines, with guns behind them that at last were quiet. I remembered many other Eleventh of November's: in London, where the multitudes stopped and stood with bowed heads as the eleventh hour struck; in villages where the scene repeated itself in miniature around the green; in small colonies abroad, when a few expatriates gathered for this annual homage in the English Church. I remembered, as the years passed, how true meaning gradually faded from this celebration, while the shadow of new war grew, and it became little more than an empty form. The course of human events led to no better future but doubled back towards the old shallows and miseries.

Now, after nearly fifty years, another Eleventh of November dawned and brought with it what sounded to me like a new note of truth. Might this be the turn in the disruptive tide? I thought of the other acts of Independence, all of them achieved only by blood, and wondered if this time reason would prevail, or England again go from folly to fiasco.

I remembered my children playing in the British trenches and on the British cannon at Yorktown. How bitter a war was that, and how long and vain a wrangle followed it. As late as 1796 Talleyrand wrote to his English friend Lord Shelburne (a friend of the Colonists):

"The only obstacle that I foresee to the rapid improvement of relations between the two countries is the incredible folly of the British Government, in doing everything that could possibly offend the susceptibilities and alienate the affections of the Americans. Their diplomatic representatives are treated with contempt in London and England is represented in America by men who are known for the fervour of their opposition to the cause of independence or else by minor officials of no importance."

Were we to go through all that again, with a Mr. Wilson playing the part of King George? We were, as the reader now knows, whose ears have heard all the uproar about "rebellion" and "an illegal act" and "restoring the rule of law" (where else in the world, these twenty years, has the rule of any law been invoked, upheld or restored? The rule has been that of war, not of law).

Here let me interpose a thumbnail sketch of a Rhodesian "rebel", for the reader's album. About seventy years ago a Rhodesian trooper, quick to go to England's side, rode behind a convoy of wagons carrying Boer women and children to safety. A woman in one wagon called that the children were hungry and the troopers must find food for them, so they rode off right and left, and found apples in an orchard, which they stuffed into their shirts and gave to the children when they rejoined the convoy. This trooper jogged along behind a wagon, over the tailboard of which leaned a little girl of some ten years, munching one of his apples. Nine years later he returned and married her. Some sixty years later their son, an Air Marshal serving as Minister of State in the British Embassy at Washington was putting on his best uniform and decorations (on November 11, 1965) when he was summoned to the chargé d'affaires, who informed him that Rhodesia had declared independence and he must declare his loyalty.

The Air Marshal answered that his loyalty was to his country, his government and The Crown. That was not enough, he was told. He must plainly declare his loyalty. His loyalty, he said, was to his country and government. His interlocutor solemnly wrote "Traitor" against his name!

American independence was the first, and Boer, or Afrikaner independence the next. My first memory in life is of seeing, from a nurse's arms, British soldiers move off from Saint John's Wood barracks to the South African war. My infant ears were filled with tales of dum-dum bullets (Boer) and infant Boer ears at the same time were filled with tales of powdered glass (British) in food: always the home-front propagandists besmirch the valour of the fighting men. The "wicked man" of those days was Oom Paul Kruger, whom I learned later to have been a genial and sturdy old farmer. When I lived in South Africa I came deeply to respect the hundred-year struggle of the Afrikaners for their independence and their eventual achievement of it after defeat in war. Today, steeled in the fire, they stand as an example in a degenerate time of a nation forged out of adversity and resolved to remain a nation. But what a waste of years and wars on England's part!

Then came Ireland, another small nation which persevered for three hundred years after Cromwell and at last won back its nationhood. Through the centuries were wars and talk of "rebels" and at the end the Black and Tans, but nothing availed. At the last, full-scale war appeared imminent. There was, as all agreed, no hope or possibility of compromise between London and "the rebels" in Ireland (as today in Rhodesia). By 1921 three British divisions were in Ireland, waiting the order to shoot. Then, quite suddenly, it was all blather: there was no difficulty at all: and the Irish delegates walked out of Ten Downing Street with Independence in their pockets (and today some of my grandchildren play happily around the shores of Dublin Bay).

And now, the fourth in the line of protestants against colonial government from distant London: Rhodesia. This was a different case. If "force" were to be used once more, to prevent a claim for independence obviously just by any moral law (as the former three were proved by time to be), the war that ensued would not be a local one, as in Virginia or the Transvaal or County Dublin, but general war, in Africa first, and then ballooning into another total war. This war, though "unnecessary" as Mr. Churchill called the last one, would not come from any chapter of errors. It would have been deliberately brought about and the true purpose (as in 1945) would only appear at its end.

To me, the theory of "unintentional" or "unwitting" follies, leading to war, is patently untenable today. The London and Washington governments must have known that by creating thirty or forty new "States" in Africa and installing them in the "United Nations" with as many votes (against America's and England's two for their 225 millions: Africa's total population is somewhere around 250 millions) they would put power of war into the hands of irresponsibles, who in the event clamoured for war as soon as they arrived there. What is more, London and Washington, by withholding their veto at any moment, could unleash these dogs of war, and they must have known that too.

Clearly we are in the period when some league *above* nations is to be set up, through war, over nations dispersed. Mr. Ian Smith and his colleagues, I saw with surprise, realized this and opposed themselves to the furtherance of the grand design.

Thus Rhodesia's Declaration of Independence was in fact a thing of "worldwide significance", affecting all of us, not a localised or limited quarrel (incidentally, cocks must have crowed in the shades when America and Ireland joined in the blockade).

The outcry that followed UDI unhappily followed the pattern of those earlier ones, of 1776, 1880 and 1916. The Archbishop of Canterbury, in the van, told the British Council of Churches that Christians should support the use of force (ah, these apostles of the Prince of Peace and Love!). Possibly murmurings were heard, for he later added that force should not be "resentfully" used, thus adding the theory of non-resentful force to the military manuals of the globe. He was stoutly upheld by four Canons of Westminster Abbey, where Kings and Queens are crowned. When other voices demurred that British soil should not be manur'd by British blood, the Bishop of Accra remarked that such talk of kith and kin was a form of "racialism", a word worth pondering by those who cherish family ties. Several other bishops joined in the warcry, and from America a Mr. Goldberg, appeared cometlike as United States representative at the United Nations, told "the misguided rebels" in Rhodesia that they should heed his warning voice "if the problem is to be solved by peaceful means and not by violence".

In the babble of bellicosity the only tranquil place, I found, was Rhodesia. While Mr. Wilson instructed the Bank of England to seize Rhodesian funds and Lloyd's to refuse payment on Rhodesian claims, and the Queen at Jamaica found in her hands a Speech from the Throne which "supported all measures which may be used to put an end to the illegal Government in Rhodesia", people in Rhodesia went placidly about their affairs, peace reigned, and the squeeze of "sanctions" was equably borne.

In earlier times such situations, broadening down from precedent to precedent, invariably ended, after the waste of wars and words, in confessions of error in London and recognition. The outer world stood aside and let the issue decide itself. Today we have the bogus concern in New York, where petty communities far distant from the matter cry that they cannot endure "the rebellion" and demand war to end it, and the London and Washington governments pretend that they must submit to this source of "international law".

While Rhodesia remained tranquil, "emergent" Africa, whence came the loudest uproar, was in a constant flux of revolt, rebellion and bloodshed. Against this background Mr. Wilson flew to Lagos, in Nigeria, to concert with other "Commonwealth Prime Ministers" measures to end "rebellion and chaos" in Rhodesia.

In former days public derision, I think, would have toppled the British Government at that juncture, for immediately after Mr. Wilson's departure the Nigerian Prime Minister, Sir Abubakar Tafawa Balewa, Knight of the British Empire, Privy Councillor of her Majesty the Queen, was murdered and left lying by a tree for some days (with his eyes gouged out, I believe). The rising had actually begun before Mr. Wilson reached Lagos and its extent has only lately become known by the evidence of mass graves. Mr. Wilson reported that "despite some of the gloomy forecasts made before I left London, the Commonwealth has emerged stronger than ever": it had been entirely devoted to Rhodesia and "the principle of one man one vote is regarded as the very basis of democracy and should be applied". The Nigerian "rebel régime" was forthwith recognised in London.

Then Dr. Nkrumah of Ghana, Privy Councillor to Her Majesty the Queen, went to his spiritual home, Communist China, and while there was deposed by the Ghanaian military (immediately recognised in London). The day before this happened *Punch*, which has developed from its "elderly party" phase into a sort of leftist pamphlet, published an article by Dr. Nkrumah which began: "When a social system becomes as diseased as that of Southern Rhodesia, a point is reached where the only alternative to constitutional change is a violent revolution". For once *Punch* made a good joke: and Dr. Nkrumah, returned to neighbouring Guinea, threatened to lead a violent revolutionary army into his native Ghana.

During all this period military uprisings (a large name for the true, tribal events) occurred in Burundi, Congo Leopoldville, Dahomey, the Central African Republic and Upper Volta, and the three southern provinces of the Sudan were in violent rebellion, claiming to secede into an independent republic. In Tanzania, once peaceful, a second revolution brewed and Zanzibar islanders suspected of complicity were shot or buried alive by the "Revolutionary Council's" gunmen. In Zambia, whence came the loudest clamour for British force to be used against Rhodesia, the Barotse people were persecuted, on the Copperbelt the Bemba tribe were resuming earlier tribal feuds, and, of course, the Communist-trained terrorists were foraying into Rhodesia.

All this happened in parts of Africa where, ten years before, an African might walk and work in peace and look for redress if he were wronged. It was the foreseeable result of forcing independence on unready groups and of encouraging terrorist-trained ones to move into the vacuum under the pretence that they "represented the people". Reason might have expected that his turmoil in Africa, which is but beginning, would cause second thoughts in London, but reason had no place in all this: only some ulterior motive can account for the attempt to force Rhodesia, the one peaceful and orderly place, into the northern chaos.

Such was the scene when this wandering scribe arrived in Rhodesia. 1 found that great argument still continued about the timing of UDI, whether the moment chosen was right, or too early, or too late. As to that, I have no opinion for I was not there and am not Rhodesian and of all glad words of tongue or pen the gladdest are these: I do not know. But from the moment of the Declaration the issue became a world one, affecting all who here on earth do dwell, and that was why and where I came in.

I found that Rhodesians are inveterate controversialists and that even when the country was engaged in a struggle of life and death they continued vigorously to dispute with each other about the colour in which the parish pump should be painted. However, in the matter of Independence, now that it was declared, they were all at one, and each new move or menace from the outer world brought them closer. If they survive, a second white nation in Africa will have been created at this point in time. Before there were people living in Rhodesia. After UDI there were Rhodesians.

Try, agile reader, to put yourself in the place of the quiet man in this quiet room, whom destiny has matched with the hour of Rhodesia's independence. You are forty-seven years of age and twenty-five years ago you, and many of the men around you, were of those to whom England, still inviolate in the silver sea, looked upward and gave thanks for island freedom preserved. You were of those to whom America too, having thought that England's day was done and that Hitler would wring its neck chickenwise, as he undertook, began to look with admiration and a changing mind. You are of those who, without a second thought, hastened from far away to fight the battle for Britain. You are Rhodesian-born but your blood and loyalty are British, and, as you once wrote, you would have to unlearn to be British than to do otherwise than you now do.

Today you are "a rebel" and the head of "an illegal régime" and invective is showered on you from the island you once helped defend, and you may ask yourself, where, oh where is loyalty bred.

Mr. Ian Smith, a quiet man in a quiet room, sits in the quiet eye of the storm, for sunwashed Salisbury outside and the lands around are peaceful and tranquil, in violent contrast to the sound and fury in Africa beyond and in London and Washington further still. Never a hard word has gone out from here.* The epithets "liar", "frightened little men" and "bunch of thugs" are those of The New Statesmanship in London. At this end of the disagreement is dignity and words are measured before they are used, which is not too often.

Provocation is ignored. What did Talleyrand say nearly two hundred years ago: ". . . the British Government is doing everything that could possibly offend the susceptibilities and alienate the affections of the Americans" (today, the Rhodesians). When I saw Mr. Smith he, in agreement with Mr. Wilson, was just about to send three negotiators to London to see if the matter in dispute could not be composed. The anonymous, and sometimes scurrilous "spokesman" in Whitehall, where "news" is "managed" nowadays,

---

*Mr. Ian Smith may have studied, for he certainly practises, old Polonius's precept: "Give thy thoughts no tongue, nor any unproportioned thought his act . . . Beware of entrance to a quarrel; but, being in, bear't that the opposed may beware of thee. Give every man thine ear, but few thy voice".

announced through the press, when they arrived, that they were "rebels under safe conduct". Even this was ignored in the quiet room where Mr. Ian Smith sits.

The Queen's portrait is on his wall there. His table is bare and tidy. A few papers lie in the familiar red box, opened before him. Here is calm. The menaces put into the Monarch's mouth brought from him only the comment, "This is a very serious matter".

If a destiny shapes our ends, it prepared Mr. Ian Smith for this hour, for everything in his life formed him to meet as grave a responsibility as ever fell on any human shoulders. I met men who knew him at school and university and their common recollection was of a *quiet* fellow to whom others turned without any exercise of attraction on his part. The gift of leadership was his, and of courage inherited from a Scottish father and strengthened by the nature and climate of the country where he was born and bred. Head Prefect at his school (Chaplin), and captain of rugby, cricket and tennis. Senior Student at his university (Rhodes), and colours for rowing, rugby and athletics. Then the Second War and the Royal Air Force.

He flew in the Desert, in Italy and on the Western Front and was twice brought down, once behind the enemy lines. He fought for five months with the Italian partisans, then escaped to rejoin the Allied forces and serve out the war. The traces of plastic surgery are still to be seen on his face.

He is about the same age as Washington when the struggle for American independence was fought. Like Washington, he is a farmer. They called it "country gentleman" in those days: well, Mr. Smith is a gentleman whose farm is in the country and, like Washington, he grows tobacco.

The difference is in the task before him. Washington had but one antagonist, the King in London and his soldiers. Mr. Ian Smith faces a rabble of demagogues who think to use the United Nations to bring the world in arms against him. What the sequel will be if he gains the day, none can yet tell. Today it seems doubtful that Washington succeeded in creating a nation in the United States, for national interest no longer governs that country's acts. Mr. Ian Smith, if his Davidian contest with the Goliath of engineered menace be won, might succeed where Washington may have failed.

His strength lies in the fact that he is not a professional politician

71

and has a population behind him which is small but staunch and determined. It is predominantly of British stock but nearly a third of it is Afrikaner. In these two groups his country has a bedrock of granite, and if it survives a splendid future lies ahead.

I have met a host of political gentlemen in my time, among them many Most Forgettable Characters, such as Hitler, Litvinoff and Mussolini, and count this meeting with Mr. Ian Smith as exceptional and memorable. I felt in him the quality of leadership remarked by others who knew him earlier and well, and which I remember encountering only once before in my life (all the officers in No. 16 Squadron, R.F.C., in 1917 felt it in a young major who in the Second War became head of the Royal Air Force, and after it was one of four resplendent figures grouped around the Queen at her coronation).

Mr. Smith is modest, disciplined and informed: as cool as if the business in hand were that of an interim board meeting: void of heat or rancour and, above all, candid and honest. He is the kind of man of whom any other knows at once that his word is his bond, words once held in high esteem in England.

When we talked the Battle for Rhodesia had reached a most dangerous point and you, encloistered reader, may be thankful that the moment passed without much worse befalling.

From Portugal Dr. Salazar the silent, who never lets words become his master, if, unspoken, they may remain his slaves, had warned the London Government that "one more false step" would set the world aflame. From South Africa Dr. Verwoerd, a master of prudence, in measured but weighty terms conveyed a similar message.

The moment of no-return was nearly on us all then, and this was one of the things we privately talked about. Another was the matter of a republic, for which some people in Rhodesia, finding the provocations too much, began to press. What he told me, on this point, was what he has publicly said, so that I may repeat it. A republic was not in his thinking at that stage. In this, I judge, he may have been a wiser head than some outside who were impatient.

The Rhodesians have an indestructible loyalty, which indeed can only be destroyed by others, for it is their birthright and pride, as once it was England's. They are true to themselves and cannot slough off this quality like a skin. Even if they were forced to declare

72

a Republic, this inmost faith would remain for long to come. If they survive, they, and their neighbour Afrikaners, may regenerate the name of the white man in Africa, and one day effect the rebirth of the old quantities in England.

I took leave of Mr. Ian Smith, a leader beleaguered and unafraid, and walked through the park nearby, where the war memorial bears seven simple words, "We fought and died for our King". Salisbury was tranquil and pleasant. The people around went their ways unhurriedly. A few empty shops and flats marked the damage done when England destroyed the great Federation at the behest of those who now clamoured for war. This, and what more might come, dismayed none: it was part of the price of survival.

In the room I left Mr. Ian Smith, beneath the portrait of the Queen, turned without haste to the red despatch box and the few papers in it. Only when I left him did I recall that this was the third time in my life that I sat and talked to a head of government, at whose door invasion bade to knock. Dr. Schuschnigg in 1938, in the Chancellery where Dollfuss was murdered: years in Nazi captivity awaited him, and then reclusion in a quiet American university. Dr. Benesh in the Hradjin at Prague: years of exile in London lay before him, and then assassination when he returned to Prague. For Mr. Ian Smith, I hoped, time had better things in store.

. . . AND OF A REBELLION!

History, as the late Mr. Henry Ford truly observed, is bunk: somebody's version of past events, tinted to taste and moulded to the historian's idea of what ought to have happened. Living history cannot be made by stitching events onto a framework of dates, any more than a skeleton can be reclothed with flesh and reanimated with coursing blood. True history is best written before it occurs and that is why I write this book about the brewing of a third world war for the purpose of setting up a World Directorate. The advantage of this method is that it can be checked. A disadvantage is that such books, at occult promptings, soon are withdrawn from shelves in public libraries. The public is not desired to enquire within on everything, only on such things as are held good for it to know, this being the purpose of "History". I like to study, with a psychopathist's interest, the image of the Hitler period in Europe which "History" has left on the mass mind. Most people now living, I suppose, experienced it, either from afar or, like myself, at first-hand, but the mental impression retained by nine folk of ten is remote from the truth of what happened: "History" has been at work on them.

Knowing well that our good old friend, The Future Historian, will not be deterred by my or any other's account from setting down his own version of events, I nevertheless want to describe the great Rebellion in Rhodesia while I am watching it.

I conjecture that the word "Rebellion" conveys a picture of violent revolt to the mass mind, especially if it is printed in capital letters. If doubt about the violent nature remains, this is probably removed when "rebellion" becomes "rebellion and chaos" (Mr. Wilson's words, I believe). The rebellion in Rhodesia, as I saw and am seeing it, presents a somewhat different picture.

One evening, six months after UDI, I sat with a gifted Rhodesian lady in a Salisbury picture-theatre. She never saw England and her heart and soul were in The Rebellion: that is, in Rhodesian independence. Nevertheless, her British blood and birthright were the most precious things in her life and not even the England of 1966 could deprive her of that heritage, which would stay with her while life lasted, whether Rhodesia were independent or not, and even if England sank below the sea. As the curtains drew apart she complained to me that the Queen's anthem had not been played. I was able to tell her (having read this in my newspaper) that other complaints had been made, that the theatre manager explained that the film of the Guards' Band playing the anthem had been damaged, and that he would soon procure another.

Continuing in search of rebellion (as Mr. H. V. Morton might say) I found myself on a day in one of Salisbury's verdant avenues, on my way to see Her Majesty's representative. His occupation gone, Sir Humphrey Gibbs was still in the Governor's mansion and his flag, the golden Crown on a blue ground, still flew there. As was to be expected, the Queen's portrait dominated his room. On the other side of the avenue, in another mansion, sat the rebel Prime Minister, head of "the illegal régime", Mr. Ian Smith. As might not have been expected, the Queen's portrait dominated his room. At the time of independence Mr. Smith referred to "this lady whom we love so much" and these words described the feelings of Rhodesians of British stock, who combined a personal devotion to the wearer of the Crown with their loyalty to the ancient monarchy as such. In some this was destroyed by the Jamaica speech, but even then it survived in most, I think, and the betrayal was separated from the speaker and laid at the door of "advisers".

I imagine that the British newspapers of this period will have received a picture of Sir Humphrey Gibbs and his vis-a-vis in that avenue, Mr. Ian Smith, as sworn antagonists, facing each other in melodramatic enmity like Montague and Capulet. The truth is other.

Sir Humphrey may be the most unpopular man in Rhodesia: so they say and they may be right. People wished that he had resigned at the moment of Independence. As to that, I would not care to have been in his dilemma, a sore one indeed for a man of honour. I did not ask him about this, because I could not expect him to speak of it, but from what others tell me I believe his choice was made at the last instant and then under certain "pressure" most difficult to withstand. (I kept my conversation with him to matters that would not embarrass and what I have to say about him here, though well founded, comes from other sources).

Sir Humphrey is another country gentleman, or farmer, with a big ranch near Bulawayo: tall, distinguished, courteous, a little tired from the burden of a task as yet thankless and efforts still unknown, the model of a breed now nearly gone: the Royal Governor.

His decision to remain, which Rhodesians bitterly resented, may prove to have been their greatest blessing. One cannot say that it *will* so prove, because the end is not yet, but it *may:* too many others, irresponsible men, have a hand in this for any optimism to be justified yet. While Sir Humphrey stayed one line remained open with London, and with it the faint possibility that the parties at either end might yet reason together.

Probably the most terrible responsibility that could be laid on one man's back was put on Sir Humphrey's when Mr. Wilson stated that he would not use "force" unless the Governor called on him to restore law and order. At that time, as London knew better than any, the Moscow- and Peking-trained terrorists in Zambia were straining every nerve to contrive some incident which could be represented, by the press, radio and television in England, as a disturbance of law and order. Imagine, good reader, whither that phrase of Mr. Wilson's could have led, had a lesser man been at Sir Humphrey Gibb's post in Salisbury.

Instead (and here again I quote others who should know, not himself) he toiled away to get some sort of discussion started, and the heat reduced. I believe he reached the point where he hinted that he could not continue *unless* this happened. This was around the time when Dr. Salazar warned London against "one more false step", and at that point "the talks" between Salisbury and London at last began. As I write, they afford at least a breathing-space and in this fateful year of 1966 any man who can help bring even that much about deserves the gratitude of mankind.

Continuing my hunt for the rebellion and chaos, I went to see another of the figures in this drama, so small in itself, so big in its importance to the world (for, as you know, well-informed reader, independent Rhodesia constitutes a grave threat to world war and for this reason is the object of the present organized attack).

In a developing situation, new expedients have constantly to be devised to maintain continuity until the new edifice of state is finally completed. Mr. Ian Smith and his men have shown extraordinary ability about this, worthy of experienced statesmen of the older school. They play it cool and long, in the modern phrase, and have never yet made a false step.

Here was the strange situation that Independence was proclaimed and at the same time unbroken loyalty to the Crown expressed, whose Ministers in turn declared the Independence Government to be an illegal one, with whom the Queen's Representative in Salisbury must have no truck. Various ways of filling this gap were considered, among them the appointment of a Regent. Had this been done the Minister for Defence, Lord Graham, might have had to fight hard not to have the honour thrust upon him, for he is in fact the Duke of Montrose, and looks it (and genealogists might determine that he is also the rightful King of Scotland). This would have produced a *tableau vivant* of Shakesperean proportions, with Scotland's famous Duke acting as Regent for a Queen whose speech-writers declared the Rhodesian government unlawful and rebellious.

The idea of a Regency paled and the problem was solved by the appointment of an "Officer Administering the Government", Mr. Clifford Dupont, whose part might be described as that of proxy for Sir Humphrey Gibbs until the issue is determined, one way or the other. He opens Parliament and delivers the Speech from the Throne in which governmental policy is outlined.

Mr. Dupont presides over another mansion, also with the Queen's portrait. In him I found another cheerful and most able man, unalarmed, with a keen legal mind and a distinguished war record in the Desert.

My memories of political gentlemen in many lands cover a long and wide range. In addition to the Most Forgettable Characters earlier mentioned, they included many worthy personages from Herren Luther and Stresemann, through Messrs. Ramsay Macdonald and John Simon, Drs. Schuschnigg and Benesh, to Messrs. Anthony Eden and De Valera and General Smuts. Thus I considered the men around Mr. Ian Smith with a practised eye and found them to be something new in my experience.

They were not professional politicians. They were all active men, not sedentary ones, mostly flat stomach'd, younger than the run of their counterparts in other countries, many of them farmers, several with exceptional war records on land, at sea and in the air, quiet in speech, candid and not evasive, and they looked you in the eye. I felt myself again among men of the kind I grew up to think of as typical Britishers, a breed which seems to have diminished greatly in England, and I found this climate rejuvenating.

These men spoke the language I understood and I felt at home. Take Lord Graham, for instance. Eton, Oxford, an agricultural degree and then to Rhodesia to farm. Then the war, and years at sea as a destroyer commander, and after that, back to farming in Rhodesia. I think his heart is in farming, but the ominous "wind of change" in London, and the threat to all that had been achieved in Rhodesia, pressed him into politics, as it pressed others whose natural bent was not that way, and now he has, under Mr. Smith, the heavy onus of Rhodesia's defence.

Consider, again, Mr. William Harper, of Internal Affairs. Here is another "rebel" who was a Battle of Britain pilot, one of those "few" whom Britain so lauded and decorated then and vilifies now. He has the courage one would expect, and a quick brain and under-tanding of the greater picture of what is truly at stake. He, too, came to Rhodesia to farm, and started at the beginning there, built his first abode with his hands, and came up the hard way. Like many of these men, he has a large family, and the spectacle of Africa to the north falling into chaos brought him, also, into the political battle for survival.

Mr. Desmond Lardner-Burke, of Law and Order, is South African-born. On him fell the brunt of the task of putting down the terror, and the obloquy from London that followed. He has the power to "restrict" persons identified with the terror, and in exceptional cases to hold in prison for a limited period. The "restrictees" have four hundred square miles where they may move freely about, are fed, clothed and housed, and may run a business if they will. His power of restriction is used with restraint. There are in Rhodesia no concentration camps such as that which President Kaunda in neighbouring Zambia (whence comes the terrorists and the loudest outcry for war) blithely announced in May 1966 that he was preparing for political opponents on a remote lake island, Chibue. This, he said, would have a stockade around the central part with "big-thighed policemen" to prevent escape: and to it would go Zambians who "misbehaved".

I found instruction in comparing these men, as I saw them, with the picture of them presented to the masses overseas. When I met

Mr. Lardner-Burke, for instance, he was receiving messages of thanks from Africans in the townships (and even the odd gift of the traditional rooster) for enabling them to sleep safe at nights. At the same time I saw a two-page "spread" about him in one of London's Sunday newspapers. A large picture of him appeared under the headlines, "Hatchet man . . . Behind his mild manner the ruthless boss of a new police state". "He looks like a benign bank manager" said the caption, "but a stroke of his pen puts hundreds in gaol without a trial". The number of persons in gaol was fifty-two, and these were dangerous saboteurs.

As to Mr. Ian Smith, whose true acquaintance you have now made, good reader, vilification knew no bounds. At this same time I read in a London daily an allusion to him, dragged by the ears into a paragraph about a rowdy election meeting at Birmingham. It spoke of "screaming yahoos" who placed themselves in "the same sub-level class as the agents of Dr. Josef Goebbels and Mr. Ian Smith who, with anything from bludgeons to blue pencils, try to eliminate all opposition".

I knew Hitler's Germany and Dr. Goebbels, the Storm Troops and the concentration camps, very well at first hand, so well, that I wrote books to warn England about them. The writer of the words just quoted knew them not, and knows Rhodesia not, unless by some fleeting visit. I consider his words as foul a calumny as could be found. Those who visit Rhodesia will never see a bludgeon, very rarely an armed policeman, and seldom a policeman at all. As to blue pencils, many an English writer could tell a tale.

Meeting these men was a rare and refreshing experience for me, and I wondered what the future held for them. Would they one day become as legendary as the men who signed the other famous Declaration (I hoped they would) and if so, would their work endure better than that of those others (for America is no longer truly "independent")? Or would they be swept away? The odds were stupendous; and yet, a few resolute and courageous men, convinced of a just cause, had often accomplished seeming miracles.

Between meeting them, I roamed around Salisbury and Rhodesia, studying the great rebellion. Everywhere the British flag still flew. In every government office hung the Queen's picture. The guns were being readied for the traditional twenty-one gun salute on her birthday.

The chamber beneath the room in which I saw Mr. Ian Smith was a replica in miniature of the House of Commons (and perhaps that was a mistake, to try and transplant Westminster ritual and customs, unchanged, to any and every foreign clime and soil). The usher, with his measured tread and chain and badge, came first, calling "Mr. Speaker" to clear the way until the little procession reached the chamber itself.

Next that grave and reverend seigneur, Mr. Speaker, wigged and gowned, and after him the Sergeant at Arms, silk-stockinged and besworded, bearing The Mace. The Government benches, where Mr. Smith and his followers sat beneath yet another portrait of the Queen: the Opposition benches, where the thirteen African Members sit. Mr. Speaker's chair, with the Royal Arms. Members, black and white, entering and bowing to the Chair: leaving, and bowing to the Chair.

All most decorous and traditional, and, you will agree, a *different* kind of rebellion.

After searching for and finding the rebellion, as I have described it, I went in search of the "police state". Mr. Wilson, in his acts towards Rhodesia, only continued what Conservative governments began, but he gave his actions so personal an imprint of rancour and vainglory that his name must forever attach to the outcome, whatever it may be, and for this reason the phrase, "Wilson's War", became current in Southern Africa.

He especially liked to call Rhodesia a "police state", and was so attached to this term that he congratulated the Liberal Mr. Jo Grimond on using it, saying that made three of them, the Conservative Mr. Edward Heath having employed it earlier (Hansard, 21/12/1965).*

In my judgment, two words have seldom conveyed so much misinformation to so many, and I am led to wonder what picture your mind, perceptive reader, received from their iteration. Does it resemble this:

"Every bank and government building is guarded day and night by machine-gun-toting gendarmerie" (a report from Conakry in "emergent" Guinea in March 1966).

Or perhaps this:

"Twenty-six determined soldiers with automatic weapons trained in one's stomach surround one as one steps off the airliner at Accra Airport" (from twice-emergent Ghana, March 1966).

Or possibly this:

"Police mustered a security force of 13,000 in the capital, including armed riot police and one thousand ———— troops. Extraordinary precautions, including the sealing of the 180-mile border were in force. Armoured cars patrolled the frontier to keep out suspected members of the ————. At sandbagged strongpoints armed police made close checks on cars crossing the frontier."

That seems a fair picture of a police state, judicious reader, and if you fit into the blank spaces which I have left the words "British" and "outlawed Irish Republican Army" you will see where it was. This Reuter message describes the precautions taken on Easter

---

*I recall that Hitler, about to invade Austria and Czechoslovakia, claimed that he merely wished to liberate oppressed Germans from "police states".

Sunday 1966 on the border between Eire and Northern Ireland (where the dogma of "majority rule" apparently stops).

Rhodesia is much bigger than England and Scotland together and is menaced on all sides, but it could not raise a "security force of 13,000 in the capital" or "seal off its four hundred miles of northern frontier. "It has one white policeman and less than three black policemen to every two thousand of its four million inhabitants, a total force of something under two thousand white and around five thousand black police. Its entire army is under four thousand strong, and of these less than one thousand are Europeans. The police go unarmed, save on some night patrol, and the visitor and the Rhodesian in the street alike very seldom even see a policeman.

In truth then, as I found in my search, Rhodesia is less a "police state" in any honest meaning of the word than any African country since Africa "emerged", and I speak from knowledge. That law and order are kept by so insignificant a force is due to four factors: first, to the seventy years of peace which the tribes have known under the white man; second, to the clamant wish of the tribes, after their experience of the Communist-sent terrorists, that this peace may continue; third, that the men who govern Rhodesia know how to live with the tribespeople; and fourth, that the numerically tiny British South Africa Police, like the Mounties in Canada, are an élite force, bred by tradition and experience to understand and deal with masses of tribesfolk in great areas of remote, wild and lonely country.

I have already given the picture of a tribal district, as visited by me. When Mr. Wilson was briefly in Rhodesia he was invited to visit, unled and unescorted if he wished, any tribal district he chose, but did not avail himself of this offer to "see for himself".

Is there any conceivable sense in which an honest man could call Rhodesia a police state, in our world of today, full half of which now lives under literally terrorist régimes? Rhodesia has "emergency laws", renewable by Parliament every three months, of the kind which England repeatedly has used in times of violence unrest. These were forced on it by the encouragement given in London and New York to the terrorists called "African nationalists" (a meaningless term in any context, let alone that of a continent containing a multitude of different, mutually antagonistic races, peoples and tribes. Are there, then "European nationalists" and "Asiatic nationalists"? Would the United States tolerate the idea of "South American nationalists"?).

Against these young, detribalized men who are spirited to far Cathay and Muscovy, for instruction in murder and arson, emergency laws were the least that was needed. They were not needed before, and could lapse at once if the incitement given these men in London and New York were stopped. If people in the West could see what has been done by them in Africa in the last few years, they would themselves rise against it, I imagine, but the massacres are hidden from them.

Little was ever heard there of the massacre of the Lumpa Sect at the very moment when Zambia, with the blessing of London "emerged" into independence: that was its birthmark. This sect was founded by one Alice Lenshina who, after a long coma brought on by illness following childbirth, said she had communed personally with God and obtained a very large following. Her achievement, near unbelievable to people who know African tribal life, was to liberate her followers from the fear of witchcraft. She ordered her adherents to destroy all the charms and practices associated with it and they would be immune. Her fame, as a woman who could confer immunity from the witchdoctors and their spells, spread rapidly and the number of her churches multiplied.

The Lumpa Church refused absolutely to have any part in politics or the campaign of violence and intimidation by which, for the benefit of London, the demand for "independence" was being supported. They resisted all attempts to force them into participation and the strife between them and the "African nationalists" became so heated that African troops, under British officers, were sent to preserve order.

This was a tragic episode in the British story because it occurred while Britain was still legally ruling. The excitement engendered among the African troops by the near approach of "Independence" was too much for them. Their officers could no longer control them as they reverted to tribal ways and went berserk. While the British officers vainly tried to stop them (one "with tears running down his face", I was told) they mowed down some eight hundred of the Lumpa people with machine-guns. Forty-five women and children were butchered in a church.

Photographs of this massacre exist but are unlikely ever to reach the outer world (similarly, the Rhodesian Government's report on the deeds perpetrated by "U.N. troops" in Katanga was withheld at London's request).

One published document exists which, if it were widely distributed in England, might at last awaken opinion there to what has happened and will happen in Africa, and so produce a restraining effect on London and New York. This book, *The Fabric Of Terror*, did achieve publication in America (the publisher, Mr. Devin Garritty, tells me that "no one in England would dare touch it").

It is an unemotional account, by a Portuguese writer, Mr. Bernardo Teixeira, of what was done along a 500-mile stretch of northern Angola on March 15, 1961, by terrorists from a communist camp across the Congo Republic border who, says Mr. Robert Ruark in his introduction, "did not hunger and thirst for freedom: they hungered for rape and thirsted for blood", massacred more than five hundred brown, black and white folk that day, from aged men and women to newborn babes and even babes unborn. The peak of obscenity was reached when living victims were bound to planks and passed through a sawmill.

The leaders of the usual "African nationalist" organization which carried out this massacre (called, in this case, the "Union of the People of Angola") were interviewed in New York four months later by M. Pierre de Vos of the leading Paris newspaper, *Le Monde*. They confirmed, and even boasted about all that was done. M. de Vos said there was proof of tortures perpetrated upon men, women and even children: "Do you deny these massacres?" "No, all that is true . . . They massacred everything". "Women and children included?", asked M. de Vos. "Yes, why deny it". M. de Vos then asked about the sawmill killings, and one of the group, "with a broad smile", said, "We sawed them lengthwise".

Nothing of this reached the mind of the outer world and the men involved continued to be courted in the corridors of the United Nations, and to pursue their propaganda there, "and in the chancelleries of those many nations which judge, for one or another reason, that they have something to gain from sailing with the African wind", says an eminent American writer, Mr. James Burnham, in his afterword to the book. He adds, "on the political warfare front impressive victories have been won, as the votes of

84

the U.N. bodies and the anti-Portuguese bias of most of the press demonstrate".

Then he says, "Not the least of the propaganda victories has been the concealment of the events of March 15, 1961".

Well, the book, with its photographs, is to be had, by those who wish to know. But as yet the Western world only hears of such things as Miss Phombeya's toe, and the political gentlemen continue to talk about the "police state" in peaceful Rhodesia.

Empires invariably pass: that is something old under the sun. The Roman Empire declined: other empires progressively decayed: some crumbled under defeat in war. The British Empire seemed until recent times to have found a new way of gradually liquidating responsibilities too heavy for it and yet maintaining strong bonds with the lands come of age and able to manage their own affairs.

The sudden decision, apparently made in some secret compact between the two political parties, to *abandon* the African possessions, immediately after a victory in war, was something new in the story of empires. It was in the nature of a fraudulent bankruptcy, rather than an honest liquidation, for long after the decision was made the white folk were being assured that Mother England never would desert them.

The first results have been seen, in the form of chaos in northern Africa, but the strangest result was that which followed after November 1965. Revolutions are said to devour their young: the spectacle of an empire devouring its young, Rhodesia, was novel in the pattern of decline.

The physical attempt to starve Rhodesia into submission, by means of warships, aircraft, seizures of money, repudiation of claims and the rest was one side of the unusual affair. The other aspect of it was to my mind more repugnant. This was the siege by words, spoken, written and illustrated.

What we now call propaganda is nothing new. It might be accounted among the oldest professions in the world, despite other claims to this seniority. A famous instance comes down to us from two thousand years ago, when "The chief priests and elders persuaded the multitude that . . ."

Ever since then the multitude has been persuaded of one thing or another, and usually to its own undoing. In our time the means of such persuasion have vastly multiplied, and only retirement into a cave can offer escape from them. Before the last war radio was added to them and during that war the audience on both sides of the battle was equally persuaded. "Juice of cursed hebona . . . and in my ears did pour the leperous distilment", said the British when

86

they heard the Rundfunk: "juice of cursed hebona . . . etc.," said the Germans when they heard the B.B.C.

After the Second War, and in good time for any third, came television, so that the multitude might be optically as well as aurally persuaded. Television encompassed almost the whole world and from this time on innumerable millions spent hours each day, on bar-stools or in armchairs, watching images on a screen, and in this shadow-show thought to see their world exactly as it goes.

Came the moment when this great apparatus of persuasion was to be turned, from England, like a swivelling weapon, against Rhodesia. "Shall kin with kin and kind with kind confound?" asked Shakespeare's Bishop of Carlisle. All that was mere racialism, said the new-age bishop already quoted. In this nutshell lie three hundred years of England's story and decline.

This war of words and flickering images was to me the strangest part of the siege of Rhodesia. I was amazed by the lengths to which the bombardment by falsehood was carried. Could this be the B.B.C., during the war dear for its reputation through the anti-Hitler world? With a shock of alarm, I looked at myself and wondered: had I stayed in England these forty-five years, not wandered the globe, would I have believed all this?

As a political writer of very long experience in many lands, and an intimate knowledge of the various methods of presenting, suppressing or distorting information, from open dictatorship and censorship down to "slanting" and insinuation in countries where "press freedom" supposedly prevails, I was astonished to find how completely the outer world's press, radio and television were sealed against faithful, factual and objective reporting from Rhodesia.

The country's stout nerves were proved by the serenity, and sometimes detached amusement, with which it suffered this new kind of beleaguerment. To an Englishman it was painful to watch. I had to believe my ears, but no longer recognized the country where I was born.

Every night the B.B.C. came on the air with "The World And Rhodesia" (the world, mark you, not Britain). The "Voice of America" joined in from various points in the globe, and was often more violent. The B.B.C. set up a station in Bechuanaland, just across the Rhodesian border, set a guard of British troops around it, and fired salvoes of persuasion into Rhodesia. From Zambia, where Dr. Kaunda repeatedly called for "force". Africans in Rhodesia were incited to kill, burn, maim and slash.

The explosive background to all this was provided by Mr. Wilson's statement that he would use force against Rhodesia if invited by Sir Humphrey Gibbs to restore law and order there. Compare that with what a speaker from Zambia said (in Sindebele) to Rhodesia on December 10, 1965: "The English troops will come if there is terrible disorder . . . That is when they will come. That is when all nations will come". (In these programmes B.B.C. news and talks were also relayed).

The B.B.C.'s French service from Mauritius (of all places) advertized in the local newspaper, *Action*, the offer of a transistor as prize for the best letter to Mr. Ian Smith or Dr. Verwoerd "to convince them that they should renounce their policies". The "best letters" were to be broadcast by the B.B.C. in French and English.

The B.B.C. and British newspapers frequently carried reports from the terrorists at Dar es Salaam, an obviously communist source and one a thousand miles distant from Rhodesia, about "riots" and "fighting" in Rhodesia. I can vouch, from my years as a foreign correspondent, that in earlier times reputable broadcasters and newspapers would not have given currency to such reports without first checking with their "man on the spot", in this case, in Rhodesia. The worst instance of this came at the very moment when, after six months, talks were at length announced to begin between London and Salisbury.

The attempt was at once made to wreck these talks by producing some incident in Rhodesia which, magnified out of all recognition (like Miss Phombeya's toe), might be presented to the listening myriads oversea as a sign that "law and order" were tottering in Rhodesia. A band of terrorists slipped across the Zambezi by night with grenades, guns and explosives. Although the Rhodesian police are so few, they were detected (helicopters are useful in this kind of country) and in a short encounter near Sinoia seven of them were killed and their cache of arms discovered. The incident only briefly disturbed the calm of a very small area.

A few days later, as the Rhodesian negotiators were packing their

88

bags for London the B.B.C. broadcast every hour on the hour between 6 and 9 a.m. the statement of "a spokesman for one of the outlawed African parties" at Dar es Salaam "that African guerilla fighters in Rhodesia have killed five policemen . . . and shot down twelve Rhodesian planes".

This is fiction without even a toe of foundation in fact: I was there and vouch for it. No policeman was killed or aircraft shot down: the district was completely calm. The B.B.C. had its own representative in Salisbury and did not check with him before broadcasting this "news" in its "World News": a telephone call to Salisbury would have shown its falsity. In fact, reports from Dar es Salaam or Zambia about Rhodesia should never be published or broadcast without verification. (In this case the B.B.C. next day gave out a casual "disclaimer": disclaimers never correct the original impression made on the mass mind).

Two instances (of many reported to me) have been verified by me, of "persuasion" by television. The Rhodesian managing director of a big international concern, happening to dine with an M.P. in Belfast, saw on television pictures of a large building burning "during current riots in one of the main cities of Rhodesia" and thought of returning at once: he said to his wife, "Things must be getting bad." Then the smoke cleared; he saw through it the name "Meikles", and realised that the picture was of the burning of Meikle's department store in Bulawayo many years before.

The daughter of the Rhodesian Minister for Law and Order, Mr. Lardner-Burke, was similarly alarmed when, in Britain, she saw pictures of "rioting in Rhodesia". Then a friend said, "What are those camels?" Rhodesia has no camels and these were pictures of rioting in the Sudan.

A leperous distilment indeed! I would like to live the day when, of the machine of persuasion as now employed from England, one might again say that it is honest, just, of good report and deserving of praise. Between November 1965 and June of 1966, as I write, there may, for aught I know, have been things true and of good report in it, but they were drowned in this thunder of persuasive falsehood, a sound which, as I listened, reminded me of the great barrages on the Somme in 1916.

I thought then that nothing could ever be more deafening, incessant and destructive. Now I am in doubt, for minds can be destroyed as well as men.

Chance alone brought me to Salisbury. I had ties elsewhere and felt no impulse to go there, thinking that it would differ only in its more recent beginnings from other of the white man's cities in Africa. The chance was fortunate (I mean, the chance of the attack on Rhodesia) for I found it the most agreeable city I ever knew, and to my taste it is the best achievement of the white man in Africa.

Totting up, I see that I have lived (that is, spent six months or more) in eight of the world's great cities (London, Paris, Berlin, Vienna, Prague, Budapest, New York and Durban) and spent shorter times in innumerable others, from Moscow to San Francisco, Warsaw to Washington, Belgrade, Sofia and Athens to Salt Lake City, New Orleans, Los Angeles and many more). Vienna I dearly loved: in Budapest and Prague I would fain have pitched my tent, but that Hitler drove me away; Durban became my home.

Of them all, Salisbury, to my great surprise, was the best for a man of my mind, and my mind is that of a townsman: I am not drawn to rural life, though I could be happy in a shack on some seashore if I had a boat. But the world's cities today are too big for a townsman of the kind I am: they become great cages, inescapable. This young, small city, Salisbury, had all that I desire in a city, and yet was not a concrete trap. You may walk out of it (but this rare pleasure may be one savoured only by me: I seem to be the last city-dweller who likes to go afoot).

Give a city a good ground plan to start, and the rest, I think, takes care of itself. It grows organically and may hope to be spared the laboured artificialities of town-planning.* Salisbury was blessed among cities when Cecil Rhodes, as they tell me, ordered that the streets must be wide enough to turn a span of oxen. I was fortunate to spend a night in Rhodes's house, the first one built (around 1898, perhaps). A photograph shows it standing alone on a slight eminence in the bare African scrub: not a tree in sight and, a mile away, a

---

*A very real peril. In Rhodesia certain town-planners, new come from the Northern Hemisphere I believe, forgot that they were in the Southern one and planned their townships the wrong way round, that is, in the way to which they were accustomed, with the industrial areas to the north and the residential suburbs to the south. In these parts the reverse is the natural order of things, as governed by climate and other factors: residential districts to the north and industry to the south.

few shacks and wattle-and-daub huts. Out of that has sprung to-day's city and Rhodes's house, which looks as if it would last for ever, now is lost among its neighbours. I wondered how, in those remote and dangerous days, he contrived to get the materials and builders for this sturdy, foursquare and attractive dwelling.

Rhodes's original ground plan saved Salisbury from the squeeze of "the accursed rent values" which has made most modern cities into places of deep ravines between high concrete cliffs, wherein the midget, man, feels himself all cabined, cribbed, confined and bound in, and produced the most spacious city I ever saw.

A good site helps a good ground plan and Salisbury was well chosen when the Pioneer Column halted here in 1890. On this roof of Africa, the high Central African plateau, you are on top of the world. Nothing is higher than you and even the tall buildings are set so far apart that they do not oppress. The land is flat, so that you may look along any of Rhodes's broad avenues, perhaps in the dawn when the traffic's blur is absent, to the end of the world, and reach up and touch the boundless sky, arching down to a man's level on every side. Here a man can fill his lungs and lift his head. At night the stars are bigger and brighter than elsewhere, presumably because you stand higher and nearer to them and there are no roof-shapes between.

Rhodes's avenues are, for me, Salisbury's especial charm. The men who made the town were generous with space in a measure I have seen nowhere else, and two span of oxen, not only one, might turn in some of these verdant places, for the green verges are often wide enough for a double line of magnificent trees. The houses, too, are set well back and apart, seldom cheek by jowl.

It is, predominantly, a white city, of spacious ways, with the tall green spires of cypresses for background almost any way you look. It is still small, and you may stroll for a few minutes between tall buildings and suddenly find you have left it behind. A city, to my mind, is always best at this stage of its growth. In our time cities get too big too quickly, and that sad day, presumably, must come for Salisbury too.

For a boulevardier of my taste and experience it is now just what a city should be, and astonishingly mellow, for its youth. In other modern cities of Africa the contrast between the old single-storey wood-and-iron buildings is often violent and displeasing, perhaps because of the lack of Salisbury's spaciousness. Here they seem to blend and nestle side by side, and are often embowered in flowers and gardens. Salisbury, too, by some means has been spared the great outcrops of shack-and-shanty settlements which disfigure other African cities. It has some, but far fewer than elsewhere.

I never expected to find a siege so pleasant. The menace was near and very real, but I shall always remember the months I spent in beleaguered Salisbury as some of the most agreeable of my wandering life.

Before we leave Rhodesia, enquiring reader, and explore the larger scene of which its beleaguerment is a part, as is the keystone to the arch, let us look back from the observation car of our departing train upon this land which has set the world agog; and see how it looks six months after Independence.

You will leave Salisbury, its tall white towers, green spires and peaceful populace, behind. As it diminishes you will pass between rich pastures and tribal lands, good farms and African villages of thatched huts, a fair land strewn everywhere with the fantastic shapes of kopjes, great rock-castles and boulders left by some convulsive surge of nature in times unimaginable. Everywhere people, black and white, going placidly about their business.

Sanctions have not weakened the spirit of the people or very much harmed them, as a whole. You have seen the shops and flats left empty by folk who went away when the Federation was destroyed. You may see an empty building where the American Information Service was until, from lofty moral indignation, it was closed when "the course of human events" led to Independence here. You may see a great oil refinery idle, because the blockade stopped supplies, and a big British automobile-assembly plant on half-time because the parts were withheld. None of this has had the ruinous effect desired. Independence has proved itself and the people are firm.

British governments, Conservative and Socialist, refused to allow this independence unless they were given "evidence" that the black folk were behind their government in desiring it. Now the evidence is conclusive. They could have had it long ago by going into the tribal lands, seeing the other "evidence", that of the terror, and testing the wishes of "the people" on the spot. They would not and continued the pretence that the men behind the terror were "the leaders of African opinion".

After six months the pretence has worn threadbare. The evidence they professed to want has shown itself, incontestably. The land has been independent six months, has faced pressures and strains never hitherto known, is quiet and orderly. "Chaos and rebellion" occur nearly everywhere else in northern Africa, but not here.

Now "Talks" have begun in London and if they do not produce

an accommodation before this book appears, that will not be the fault of any in Rhodesia. From the moment of UDI Mr. Ian Smith repeatedly said he was ready to talk at any time, without pre-conditions. These offers fell on stony ground. At one point, a European country was willing to act as mediator, and that method of conciliation too was rejected. If London ultimately agreed to these talks, the reader has seen why.

And now, what will the harvest be? If this were in truth just a dispute between "colonial rebels" and a Mr. Wilson, cast by mischievous prank of time for the part of King George in a revival of an earlier Comedy of Errors, the end of the play would be foreseeable: recognition and confession of error from London.

It is much more than that. Rhodesia is the present stumbling block in the way of the furtherance of the great design for World Government. For that reason the name "Rhodesia", whatever comes next, long will occupy the headlines, and the machine of public persuasion continue to distort the news about it in the columns beneath them.

These six months brought me, at least, the greatest experience of a wandering writer's long trek through scenes of trouble and tribulation, for when was ever seen so strange a siege as this, from Troy to Paris? British soldiers on the western border, guarding a radio station beamed against Rhodesia. British aircraft on the northern border, where terrorists beam their incitement against Rhodesia. And on the East . . .

If Lord Nelson did not turn in his grave (and Captain Horatio Hornblower quit his quarto-deck) at the sight of the British Navy, of glorious tradition, toiling to starve Rhodesia into submission, then at least there was a coincidental symbolism in the fall of Nelson's statue in Dublin (as in that of Rhodes's boulder), even though Irish Republicans caused this.

About that time, good urban and suburban reader far away, another war breathed down the necks of us all. The British Navy stopped a Beira-bound oil-tanker on the high seas. What would have followed if its master had refused to stop? Would the warship have fired? On an *oil* tanker?

Another tanker slipped through the blockade and reached Beira. At that point Mr. Wilson, who had said specifically that he would not "alone" call for a naval blockade of Beira, applied to the body in New York for leave to start a naval blockade of Beira, and that moment of untruth was nearly the moment of no-return.

Then Dr. Salazar warned against "one more false step" that would kindle a great flame. Combined paratroop manoeuvres were being carried out in England under the code-name "Exercise Lifeline". Here let me tell you, good reader, something which you will not know, or at any rate very few among you will know. Dr. Salazar, whose information is usually of the best, said he believed these troops were being made ready to land at Beira. He forthwith ordered reinforcements of troops and aircraft to Beira and gave his warning. At the same time he asked Mr. Ian Smith, for the sake of peace, not to offload the oil, and Mr. Smith, unwilling to leave a neighbour in such a dilemma, reluctantly but amiably agreed. These two men may have averted grave things at that time.

Whether Dr. Salazar was well or ill informed, one cannot know, but the incident shows the great dangers inherent in the "ridiculous situation" produced by London's actions against Rhodesia. A fortnight later the news-managing "spokesman" in Whitehall "scornfully dismissed" the rumours about contemplated military action at Beira. I doubt (but cannot check this) whether these rumours reached British readers, listeners or viewers, and if they did not, perhaps he protested too much. In any case, and sad to say, denials from London by then were a somewhat devalued currency in the world. Had not Mr. Wilson denied that he would ever blockade Beira?

This was the third time that England came near being embroiled in war through its actions in Africa. The episode of the "defensive bombs", proffered for use in Katanga and then withheld, I have related. The other incident occurred in 1961, when the great Federation began to crack under British pressure. Sir Roy Welensky then learned of a concentration of British troop-carrying aircraft at Nairobi, and believed that they could only be intended for use in effecting such political changes in Northern Rhodesia as London desired. He took steps to put radio beacons out of action, obstruct runways, and have smallarms fire in readiness if any aerial ingress were attempted.

Dining with Mr. Macmillan in London, later, he mentioned this matter. He says, "The tears rolled down Macmillan's cheeks. 'Roy, do you really believe that I, who have seen the horrors of two world wars, would have tolerated a situation in which Britishers would have been shooting down Britishers, their brothers, alongside whom they have fought on many a battlefield?' 'Before you go any further, Harold' (cut in Sir Roy) 'you'd better understand that I sent a Canberra up to Nairobi last month. I know you were gathering troops and aircraft there. Where else in the world were you going to use them except against us?' 'But of course', he sighed, 'of course, Roy, we all make mistakes. Those aircraft and troops weren't to be used against you. We were collecting them in case you needed them, and we should have had them there ready for you'."

Dr. Salazar, as may be seen, was not vapouring when he warned against "one more false step", or foolishly panicking when he ordered troops and aircraft to Beira.

By mid-1966 not one truly stable state remained in northern Africa, of the many newly-created in the preceding few years. The shambles foretold by Lord Salisbury, and for that matter by every competent and unprejudiced observer, many years before was spreading all the time.

In Uganda, a "fully independent member of the Commonwealth" for nearly three years, the old tribal wars burst into flame. The President, a Mr. Milton Obote, abrogated the constitution bestowed by departing Britain, under which Uganda, on paper, became a federal republic of its four provinces, with the central and chief one, Buganda, retaining an especial status under its Kabaka, or king. He deposed the Kabaka from the Ugandan presidency, and made himself president. The Kabaka thereon told Mr. Obote to remove his government from Buganda soil, and Mr. Obote thereon sent troops to attack the Kabaka's palace. Fierce fighting followed and the numbers killed may one day become known, though I doubt this. Sir Edward Frederick Mutesa, Knight of the British Empire (the Kabaka), a former Grenadier Guards officer affectionately known as "King Freddie", escaped and eventually reached England.

In Kenya, next door, the paper constitution and the incomprehensible (to the African mind) idea of one-man-one-vote seemed to be on the way out, as President Kenyatta's ruling party pressed hard for a one-party state with "preventive detention" powers. In Nigeria, whence Mr. Wilson emerged in January saying that the

"Commonwealth leaders" there were agreed that one-man-one-vote was the very basis of democracy, the rebel régime which took over on his departure announced in May, through its military head, General Ironsi, that all political parties were abolished and that "the army" would remain in power three years.

But for the rising toll of blood, the thing would have turned into pure *opera bouffe* in May when President Kaunda of Zambia, in a shrieking speech at Lusaka which included several references to the "idiots" in London, announced that he would propose the expulsion of Britain from the Commonwealth unless the Rhodesian Government were promptly removed by it: he could not endure the continuance of rebellion there. At this a Mrs. Judith Hart was sent to Lusaka to placate him: a new figure on the troubled scene (though well known to members of the "Movement for Colonial Freedom", a body which often embarrassed the Socialist Party, in earlier days, by its activities) she was now, the newspapers said, "Minister of State for Commonwealth Relations". As to these relations, one learned at this moment that a Mr. Arnold Smith was "Secretary-General of the Commonwealth Secretariat" and he, too, continued to be deeply concerned about the issue of "racialism in Rhodesia", which, he said in far Ontario, might break up the Commonwealth. The "great potential value" of this institution, he said, was that "it represented a cross-section of humanity, races, ideologies and creeds". He was right: very cross.

Unhappily, the *opera bouffe* had a bloody background. The terrorists from Zambia were evidently instructed to change their unsuccessful tactics when they slipped over the border into Rhodesia and to concentrate on lonely white farmers in isolated homesteads. Two of these were shot through a window just before Mr. Kaunda spoke, and he made inflammatory references to the murders, for instance, that "more innocent people" were likely to die as the result of "the explosive situation in Rhodesia".

Then, as earlier, no explosive situation existed *in* Rhodesia: the only explosives were those brought into it from Zambia by the communist-trained terrorists.

Yet in the House of Commons Mr. Bottomley, questioned about this matter, attributed it to UDI, until he was shouted down by indignant Members, when he retired into the worn formula that he was against violence from any quarter. The reader will remember that the terrorists were active long before UDI, that Mr. Bottomley was repeatedly begged to satisfy himself of their external origins and masters, and that he continued to the end to allude to them in respectful terms as representing "African opinion".

Similarly, in the House of Lords Lord Salisbury asked whether the government would condemn such incitements to murder as President Kaunda's reported words on May 12, 1966, that "blood has got to be spilled" to oust the Rhodesian government. Lord Longford, the government spokesman there, dragged out again the hideous cliché about the government "opposing violence from whatever quarter", and being pressed to say whether this applied to the particular case in point (Mr. Kaunda's words) said he would not "pass criticism on the head of a friendly Commonwealth country" (Mr. Kaunda's country, lest the reader be in doubt). Lord Salisbury said, "That second answer will be regarded by many people in this country as condoning violence, and even murder". This writer certainly so regards it.

In this darkling scene of manmade confusion and evil, where London and New York seem witch-bent on making a brew of powerful trouble, things that are true, honest, just, pure, lovely, of good report, virtuous and deserving of praise are few and hard to find. The faithful scribe, however, must seek them out, and here I show the other, better side, where some promise may be discerned of a return to peace, stability and order in tormented Africa.

If Rhodesia's independence is maintained, there are the makings of a strong group of "States" in the true sense of the word in Southern Africa, three of them strong and self-supporting in themselves, and three neighbouring weaker ones moving in the orbit of the greater. Together this group would give Africa a firm basis of order, stability and improvement which in time would project its influence into the present northern confusion and exert a stabilizing influence there.

The three small British protectorates in or near South Africa and Rhodesia, Swaziland, Basutoland and Bechuanaland, always feared to be engulfed by South Africa. Today their fears are quite other. They see, on the one hand, murder and mayhem everywhere in the north, and, like the Africans in Rhodesia, fear that more than any other thing on earth, for they, with tribal "history" living in them, know just what it means. On the other hand, they see order and progress in Rhodesia and South Africa, and in South Africa the policy of separate native homelands (Bantustans) which greatly appeals to them. These organic processes of development attract them much more than the prospect of tribal and other war offered by the chaotic north. Also, they already feel the near presence of the terror from Dar es Salaam and Lusaka, and have within their own communities men who would like through terror to become such "Messiahs" as Dr. Nkrumah once in Ghana.

Therefore all three of them, through their heads, Mr. Seretse Khama of Bechuanaland, Chief Jonathan of Basutoland and Prince Makhosini Dhlamini of Swaziland, have announced that when independent they will pursue "policies of a healthy, good understanding with neighbour states" and of non-interference in the internal affairs of other countries. Chief Jonathan, an enlightened man, once remarked that Africa had "become a laughing stock in the world" through events in the north.

Then in Malawi, on the other side of Rhodesia, Dr. Hastings Banda, who played the chief part in wrecking the Federation and today might regret that, looking at the chaos around has repeatedly spoken against "force" and for constitutional ways. He seems at the moment to have mellowed greatly and enjoys increasing prestige among men white and black. He recently spoke to his parliament at Zomba in words which true men for years have vainly hoped to hear from London and Washington:

Childish resolutions were proposed at the United Nations and at the Organization for African Unity. "I have my own ideas. I am not going to vote in a certain way just because I am an African. When they do the right thing, then I agree. When they do the wrong thing, I do not agree. Other Prime Ministers follow what their friends do. If I think my best friend is wrong, then I disagree with him. Those who are calling the tune are not in a position to pay the piper. Too many ignorant people are in power in Africa today. That is the tragedy of Africa, and that is why Africa is in a mess."

There speaks truth, but the "ignorant people in power" are not only in Africa: there's the real rub.

Dr. Banda has extended this advice personally to Africans from other countries and, as his repute is high, this has had effect. In Rhodesia the leader of the 13-man African opposition in the

Salisbury Parliament, Mr. C. Chipunza, also interjected a word of wisdom into the great argument. He advised leaders of black African States against interference in Rhodesian affairs and particularly against harbouring exiled terrorists in their countries. This advice, clearly directed first and foremost to Mr. Kaunda in Zambia, goes to the very root of all evil, the one which British Ministers, from Messrs. Macmillan and Sandys to Wilson and Bottomley, refused to see or know.

Mr. Chipunza's words (may they at last be heeded in London and New York) are those of a statesmanlike politician:

"What this country needs for a solution of its problems is the co-operation of all reasonable Rhodesians, white and black, towards the eventual creation of a non-racial State. This can and must be achieved. But the delay or prevention of such achievement is caused as much by the extremism of African leaders to the north as by extremist white politicians in Rhodesia itself. What our situation calls for above all else is statesmanship by all parties concerned. The leaders of other African states are not directly concerned and their interference is both unwarranted and unhelpful."

With these words of truth, rare in a time when the great machine of public persuasion works at top speed to make the multitude think differently, let us, friend reader, take a last look at Rhodesia, stable and peaceful, from our observation car, and fare forth into the outer world, where all the trouble has been engineered.

When you cross Beit Bridge, good reader, you will leave Rhodesia behind and from your observation car see another country around you, also a thriving, stable and improving one. Consider it well for, between you and me, this country, not Rhodesia, is the real object of the exercise which I have described. Rhodesia is a hindrance between our One Worlders and the place they really thirst to get at: South Africa. It is the last bastion of white nationhood.

My first memory in life is of being held up to see British troops move off to South Africa. That was in the time of the great Queen, whose oleograph may even today be seen in an African hut or two in the bleak mountains of Basutoland. Then in the First War I found myself alongside South Africans, of Afrikaner and British stock, in the trenches and the flying corps: I remember burying what remained of one, in a blanket, somewhere near Lens.

In the Second War I met a notable Afrikaner, Colonel Deneys Reitz, who killed his British trooper in the South African war and fought beside the British in the next one. His book, *On Commando*, gives the picture of a Christian soldier, fearless and irreproachable. He came to believe in Empire and was not beloved by many of his fellow Afrikaners, who deeply distrusted Britain and the purposes behind our Twentieth Century wars.

That was about all I knew of South Africa, until 1947. Today I find that if I live as long as most of my progenitors* I shall have spent more of my years in Southern Africa than anywhere (for I have passed only the Second War years in England since I went to the first one at nineteen).

When the Second War ended a happy instinct took me away from the returning inertia of England and to South Africa. There I met General Smuts, the commando leader of 1900 who became an outstanding figure of Empire. He played a great part in many

---

*A longlived and disputatious clan. In America once I found "Reed" on so many stones in a Connecticut churchyard that I made enquiry and learned that the sire of them all was a Roundhead colonel, John Reed, who left my own West Country for America rather than submit to King Charles's restoration. A hundred years later Reeds were still divided on this issue. A dozen Reed patriarchs, descended from him and mostly aged around eighty or ninety, met to debate the rebellion of the Colonists. About half of them decided to join it and the others took boat for Canada, there to live under the King.

great events and his name and fame were universal (save, as I soon found, in South Africa).

Full of years, honours and acclaim, Rembrandtesque in feature, he looked darkly into the future as he talked to me. Until then I thought of South Africa as a fortunate isle, spared the direct hand of world war, free, abundant in natural wealth, a mine of opportunity. At that instant I dimly felt that this was not quite so. The elder statesman, renowned in every capital of the world, a bestarred and bemedalled field marshal (the Boers disliked that, who thought of war in terms of their everyday clothes and broad-brimmed hat, a horse, a gun and a bit of biltong), the intimate of great councils in London and Washington, here at the Cape of Good Hope was not sanguine but somewhat careworn.

I saw him again when he spoke to a crowd in Durban. From long experience I can feel the mood of a crowd. These people were unresponsive to the world statesman. I thought then that the great man's day was nearly done. It was: a little later I watched election results in a cinema and saw that he was defeated on his home ground. I was in British Natal then and around me was an uneasy stir. These folk read in the eclipse of the champion of Empire and reconciliation the approach of all they feared.

That was in 1948 and in the following years I watched the Afrikaners, whose chief recreation is the discussion of politics, prove themselves highly skilled and tireless organizers. They went from strength to strength until their control of the country was complete. This was not entirely their own achievement. It was largely due to the British abandonment of Africa. From Kenya, Uganda, Tanganyika, and after the destruction of the Federation, from Rhodesia, white folk came to South Africa, as once British armies to Dunkirk. From this Dunkirk, however, there would never be any thankful relief by small boats. This was a last ditch.

Such people, deserted by their homeland, turned to the Afrikaner government. As the northern turmoil grew, even the British in Natal began also to turn that way. When Rhodesia took independence and was at once besieged and threatened with invasion, this gradual movement became a surge, and in 1966 Dr. Verwoerd and his men gained an electoral victory which showed that Natal, too, now stood with them.

In twenty years British governments, chiefly Conservative but

103

headed at the decisive moment by a Mr. Wilson, laid the foundations of two white nations in Africa. Before, there were no "Rhodesians", only people living in Rhodesia, most of them deriving their heart's blood from England and giving it back in a uniquely staunch loyalty. Today a Rhodesian nation is in the throes of birth. Similarly, a South African nation of Afrikaners and British-descended South Africans is coming into being.

These two communities are strong enough together to overcome many a sea of sorrows; at any rate, another total war would be needed, in my estimation, to reduce them. As to that, we were on the verge in April and May of 1966 and for the moment a reprieve is probably all that can be counted on.

The common cause produced by the menace from the chaotic north has, on the long view, a basic flaw. The instinctive movement of the white folk in Rhodesia towards South Africa and of the British in South Africa towards the Afrikaners is a negative, not a positive one. It is the mutual reaction to a common danger, not a conversion of minds. In the matter truly at issue, the survival of white nationhood in southern Africa, a gulf is still fixed between two ways of thought. If this continues, even an established independent Rhodesia would only mean a respite, leaving the gap through which the international mob, crying Havoc, would through Rhodesia one day descend on South Africa.

The Afrikaners, absolutely devoted to the survival of their nation. have evolved a practical way of ensuring it among the black folk, The Rhodesians are for the nonce caught up in the delusive theory of "racial partnership" which binds them, under the usual made-in-London constitution, to a process leading to the opposite: black domination. By that path they can gain only time, not survival. At its end, the all-black state would arise on South Africa's border and the breach be opened for the final assault.

At this point, allow me to explain, truth-seeking reader, that the Afrikaners are the *only* nation in Africa, unless the Egyptians may now be so classed again. They have been here for over three hundred years and in 1806, when the British took over the Cape, were cut off from their imperial mother-country in Europe. Then they moved away, far inland, to breed a new, separate nation, born in adversity and now with its own language, tradition and birthright. They are Africans: a white nation rooted in African soil.

104

Nothing will induce them to surrender this birthright, but since General Smuts was defeated in 1948 they have devised a practical means of ensuring separate peace and separate freedom for black and white people, both. They already had within their borders two tribal enclaves, Swaziland and Basutoland, British dependencies which are now moving towards independence and are committed to amicable relations with surrounding South Africa. They have created a third out of their own territory, the Transkei, which has been fully self-governing since 1963, under complete black supremacy (its leaders will have no truck with "racial partnership" and are not desired to).

This "Bantustan" method will be continued. In South Africa it is practicable because the large tribal areas are fairly plainly outlined, for instance, "Zulustan".

I now know a little of Africa and judge that this is the only way of enabling white and black people to live together in one territory in a relationship of mutual respect and betterment, while ensuring the survival of white nationhood.

As to white nationhood, a man who watches South African and Rhodesian children on the beaches, on the farms and in the mountains, may see that it is still the great race, having more to offer the world than another for long to come. This, to the vituperators of London and New York, is "racialism" and anathema, but it is the truth and their motive is an ulterior one.

The Rhodesian case is different. For Rhodesia too the survival of white nationhood is an imperative: for that, in truth, it has faced the world, alone, in 1965 and 1966. Anything less would be vanity: a palliative and not a cure; a stay of execution ending with submergence in the northern chaos. The difficulty in Rhodesia is that, although the tribes own more than half the land, this is scattered in pieces over the map. The Bantustan method therefore is less simple to apply, and delicate surgery would be needed gradually to achieve the white homeland and the black homeland under white control. If it were done, Rhodesia would become a stable neighbour of South Africa and stability in Southern Africa would be re-assured. Unless some such rearrangement be effected, even Independence, in the long run, would prove illusory.

The Afrikaners perceive that chink in the armour. Despite their prudence in international affairs (Dr. Verwoerd has shown himself

105

to be one of the very few statesmen remaining in the world) they are a far cry from the hub of international machinations, and were taken by surprise by the fury of the assault released against Rhodesia. It jolted them into realization of their own endangered position in the world. The Afrikaner is not easily perturbed and long shrugged off the outer world's ravings and railings as the verbal outpourings of "Liberalism", which from every instinct he despises. He suddenly saw the wolfish fangs behind the sheepish mask, and knew then that menaces which he thought theoretical and distant were perils real and near.

Liberalism! The word is used today as the wolf wore Red Riding Hood's grandmother's nightcap, and the motive is the same. I sought it in the dictionary and found that it originally meant "becoming a gentleman". This meaning is described as "now rare", and I would imagine might be called obsolete. Later, it came to denote a person of generous and open-minded spirit in all things. Finally, it signifies today one who is "favourable to constitutional changes" and there you have it. That definition, by the cumulative and overwhelming evidence of our century, covers revolution, assassination, the one-party state, invasion (does not the cry of Havoc and Force come from our Liberals?), bully-boys with automatic weapons, the lot.

Liberalism today is a cover-name for every purpose that is destructive of nationhood, familyhood, (both of these are now "racialism" in the Liberal vocabulary), religion, liberty and peace.

Let us now, good friends and neighbours, consider what Liberalism has in store for South Africa, and the part played in it by good old Andrew Carnegie, who also might writhe in his tomb if he could see what is being brewed in his name.

BLUEPRINT FOR BATTLE

When Scottish-bred men, among others, were pushing the moving frontier westward in America, and Scotsmen, among others were pushing it northward into Rhodesia, young Andrew Carnegie from Dunfermline was amassing great wealth in America. As he grew older his fortune increased until it was almost beyond computation. He was a great man and a good one. His benefactions were innumerable and many of them were given in directions which, he thought would help to promote peace in the world. This vision of peace was indeed uppermost in his mind. Among many other things, he was among the first and most generous in contributing to the erection of a Temple of Peace at The Hague. (Whether this survives, I know not: if it exists, possibly a little peace may be found within it; in that case, it is a rare sanctuary in our contemporary world).

The Book tells us that a camel may easier pass through the eye of a needle than a rich man enter heaven. Even more difficult, perhaps, is it for a rich man to ensure that his money, which he may not take with him, shall promote purposes dear to him, for instance, Peace.* Old Andrew, who by good intention qualified for unchallenged entry into heaven, did what mortal man can do to make sure that when he died (in 1919) his dollars should help establish that enduring peace in the world which he and all true men devoutly desired.

To that end he founded the Carnegie Endowment for International Peace, and the world applauded this magnificent bequest, which in ensuing years developed so many noughts behind the original figure that it grew into treasure beyond the understanding of that common man who is the darling of our age.

Therefore, good people, let us now look with pleasant anticipation at the Carnegie Foundation's work for peace, as manifested in 1965.

Where there's a will there's a way of reversing its intention. The

---

*For general information on this fascinating subject, in a non-political context, I commend the chapter The Founder's Intention, in Mr. Nubar Gulbenkian's autobiography *Pantaraxia*. This describes Mr. Gulbenkian's nine-year struggle to have the funds of the Gulbenkian Foundation administered according to what, in his opinion, was his father's intention.

Carnegie Foundation in 1965 (forty-six years after its founder's death and a few weeks before the assault on Rhodesia) published, and distributed to all 114 representatives of the United Nations in New York (whose equanimity it disturbed not at all) a 170-page book entitled "Apartheid and United Nations Collective Measures" which contained a blueprint, worked out to the last detail, for an attack on and invasion of South Africa.

The introduction contained an expression of thanks to an officer of the "Department of Social Sciences"* at the Military Academy at West Point (the American equivalent of Britain's Sandhurst) for his help in planning "U.N. military measures necessary to achieve the goal of transforming the South African social and political structure".

The detailed estimate of the forces necessary includes 30,000 assault and 63,000 other troops: 145 warships, transports and supply vessels and 300 aircraft: and 200 transport aircraft requiring "3,000 total flying hours for direct assault". The cost of a 30-day attack by 93,000 ground troops with air and naval support is estimated at $95,000,000. The document is a highly professional product, plainly the result of long experience, research, work, and thought by persons devoted to the aim of achieving war through the United Nations. The *Chicago Tribune*, in reporting it, said that "according to reliable sources, it carried the approval of U Thant, the U.N. Secretary General.†

The Carnegie Endowment, being tax-exempt as a body promoting good works, is in fact subsidized by the American Government. A foreword to the Battle Plan, supplied by the Foundation's president, a Dr. Joseph E. Johnson (formerly of the U.S. State Department) stated that the reason for its issue was our dear old friend, the "explosive situation" in South Africa. (You, good reader, having destroyed your newspaper, television set and radio, know this to be rubbish).

---

*I always wondered what went on at these faculties "of social sciences" introduced in our time at many universities. Now I feel that I begin to have an inkling.

†This is made credible by the television interview given by U. Thant in 1966, when he called for South Africa to be blockaded by sanctions. Questioned about the war in Vietnam, then in progress, he said the U.N. had no jurisdiction in that quarter. A few weeks later the Kabaka of Uganda called for U.N. intervention when he was deposed as President of Uganda by the Prime Minister there, Mr. Milton Obote, who then made himself President. No reply was given, and when the Kabaka's palace was attacked, burned and looted by Mr. Obote's troops, a "spokesman" at the U.N. said that U. Thant could do nothing as the matter was "an internal affair".

Two other contributors to the Battle Plan are also former State Department officials, and one of them is still an "adviser" of it. The Endowment itself is now under the dominant influence, through its officers and trustees, of the U.S. Council on Foreign Relations, a body nominally private which has come to be regarded by many Americans as a shadow State Department and invisible government of the United States.

This Council appears to work closely with the African Affairs Bureau of the State Department itself, which has long been in conflict with the responsible heads of the State Department (at this moment Mr. Dean Rusk and his Under Secretary, Mr. G. Hall) on the issue of using "force" against South Africa. Its efforts resulted in a group of ten Congressmen and three Senators going to London in May 1966 to "press for more liberal U.S. policies in Africa".

One purpose of this "Liberal group" (said the Liberal *New York Times*) was to strengthen the hand of those United States officials "who believe that an imaginative, even aggressive policy of support for black aspirations is necessary", to which end they were prepared to risk conflict with "economic, military and diplomatic interests". "The Liberal outlook" of this group, added the paper, "has its origin in the African Bureau of the State Department, which often feels itself ignored by top-level officials". However, it continued, Mr. Arthur Goldberg, the U.S. Ambassador at the United Nations, "has proved a staunch ally to the Africanists" (I quoted earlier Mr. Goldberg's menaces addressed to Rhodesia).

The "Liberal outlook" of all these gentlemen is presumably indicated by the Carnegie Battle Plan against South Africa.* The Battle Plan appeared just before Rhodesia declared independence.

---

*The American public, like the British one, is prevented by various impediments from learning authentic information about Southern Africa. For instance, a three-man delegation from America which visited Rhodesia in January 1966 (Congressman Ashbrook, Dr. Max Yergan, a South African Negro, and Mr. Ralph de Toledano, a wellknown author) stated that "important publications have been told that the Rhodesian Government is not admitting accredited journalists, a totally false charge". These enquirers found that the Rhodesian Government "commands the virtually unanimous support of the white population and the respect of a preponderance of Africans". Similarly, an American judge who visited Rhodesia in April 1966 said he was told by the State Department before he left that communism was developing in Rhodesia: "From my experience and the information I have picked up here, that statement was unwarranted. There is no likelihood that conditions here could lead to a communist takeover and it is impossible for me to believe that this could happen".

Similar interferences with information about South Africa and Rhodesia occur in London.

As to the Carnegie Endowment, it might be significant that Mr. Alger Hiss, later convicted of perjury for denying his activities on behalf of Soviet espionage, was once its president.

The South African population was told little about it at the time (the leading newspapers are foreign-owned and "Liberal") and for that reason not much heed was taken of it. The attack on Rhodesia shocked Afrikaners into realizing that it must be taken seriously.

The Battle Plan even set a time for the attack on South Africa, saying that if the International Court of Justice at The Hague (you remember, dear reader: the place where the Temple of Peace is, or was) ruled against South Africa on the South West Africa issue, the American Government would probably support United Nations action "to enforce the ruling". Proceeding from this, it suggested that American Negroes could exert pressure on the American Government in this direction, and "bring interest in the situation in the South to a level seldom achieved by any foreign policy issue", by identifying their civil rights campaign in America with the Liberal call for an attack on South Africa.

The World Court's judgment will probably come before this book appears, and therefore may provide the next moment at which "one more false step" could set the world ablaze. I believe that mass Negro demonstrations (Liberal ones, of course) are being organized for that day, so that you, well-informed reader, will be able to see what transpires.

So now we come to South West Africa, on our excursion through the scenes behind the scenes. Climb again into our observation car, observant reader, take a last look at South Africa, peaceful and prosperous, and come with me to this harsh, arid and bitter place where the desert reaches down to the dangerous sea, where the whales wallow, flamingo flock and the fins of sharks slide through the surf. Here is a lonely, little-inhabited place indeed.

South West Africa! Who ever thought, or even heard of it until our Liberal One-Worlders saw in it a place where war might be unleashed.

It was a scrap thrown to the Kaiser in 1884 to appease his colonial ambitions and his envy of his grandmother's farflung possessions across the sea. The old Governor's residence still stands in forlorn Swakopmund, and the statue of the German warrior outside it. You may still take *Kaffee und Kuchen* in the little tearoom: still drink German beer in the restaurant: a few flowers have been wrung from the reluctant sand: and in the bandstand, for all I know, perhaps *am Sonntag Abend die Dorfmusik* still plays. For the white folk

110

here are mostly Germans and once, driving across the desert, I most unexpectedly encountered another traveller, driving a truck to Walvis Bay, who stopped and hailed me with "Ach, Herr Reed, ich erkenne Sie wieder". This was a German whom I briefly met in a Cape Town-bound ship.

One of the strangest experiences of my writer's life befell me in this desert. I turned aside from the recognizable road and followed a track, sometimes visible and sometimes vanished, which brought me over a hillock of sand into, of all things, a green and thriving farm of trees, flowers, fruit and vegetables, with a homestead set in it. The explanation of this seeming miracle was that the place lay in a dry river bed which collects enough moisture from the rare rains to keep the soil fertile. A disadvantage of this idyll is that the still rarer heavy rain may, and once did turn the dry course into a raging torrent, which sweeps away farm, farmstead and all. When I was there I was given good Viennese coffee and *Apfelstrudel* and, beneath the furious sun, thought of the Ringstrasse and the Cafe Bristol . . .

This is still Germany, for all that the white folk long ago became British subjects and are now South African ones. In Swakopmund the German barracks still bears the German regimental badges, and in the *Kneipe* opposite I thought to hear the echoes of clinking beermugs and of *Trink', trink', Bruederlein, trink'*.

What is South West now? A land of 500,000 people, black and white, with good cattle country far inland, fish for the catching in the sea, and diamonds along the coast. So mighty is the Diamond Empire that this coastal strip is guarded and patrolled like a king's treasure chamber, lest any beachcomber pick up an odd gem or two.

The South Africans took it from the Germans, at the cost of a few skirmishes, in the First War, and after that war it was entrusted to South Africa under "mandate", which entailed periodical reports to the old League of Nations. There were three classes of Mandate, A, B and C, and South West fell into the C category,* which came nearest to virtual transfer. The C Mandates were those which could "best be administered under the laws of the Mandatory *as integral*

---

*I believe this is the only one of all the Mandates in which the outer world, as instructed by its mass-persuasion machine, has ever taken any interest whatever. The Palestine Mandate, a British one, ended after the Second War when the Zionists from Eastern Europe with American support, drove out the indigenous Arabs. This action received the unanimous approval of the United Nations and that was, indeed, one of the first acts of this body.

111

parts of its territory" (my italics) "subject to safeguards in the interests of the indigenous population".

The indignant population, according to our Liberals, now thirsts for release from this thrall. The indignant ones are the Hereros, who form less than a tenth of the 500,000 population. They were discovered some years ago (I believe the chief discoverer was a Liberal cleric, subsequently requested to depart from various countries where he sought a Cause) and in the sequel Ethiopia and Liberia, none other, desired the World Court to rule that South Africa had violated the obligation to "promote to the utmost the material and moral wellbeing and the social progress of its inhabitants".

In an earlier act of our *opera bouffe* the old League of Nations (a less bogus outfit than the present one in New York) found, through its Slavery Commission, that slavery still survived in Ethiopia (then Abyssinia) and Liberia. Don't look now, good reader, but this is still the case.

Thus, in the current act, the world will find "South West Africa" loom large in the headlines, on the television screen, and in the broadcasts. The readers, viewers and listeners should make the most of the opportunity for thereafter they are likely to hear as little about South West Africa as they ever heard before.

In the realm of truth the case is different, again. The South African Government has pursued large and costly development schemes in South West, for the benefit, among others, of the Hereros. In the old "native township" at Windhoek, made of flattened oil cans and drums, the Herero leader, Mr. Clement Kapuuo (he is not the Herero Chief, but Hosea Kutako is 96 years old and dwells quietly in a Herero reserve) lives in his little store among sacks of meal. He and his followers refuse to move into the modern township built at the other end of the city. He has a keen politician's mind and knows his present abode to provide a scene more attractive to Liberal opinion in the distant world. As to that, he is confident that "international justice" will prevail and that South Africa will be "forced" to withdraw.

That brings us back to the Carnegie Battle Plan: the political music goes round and round and the menace of war always comes out there. Soon the Rhodesian matter may, or may not, be settled or shelved. Let none relax. Soon will come the International Court's judgment, and if it be what Liberal Opinion desires the welkin again will ring with cries of "force".

Whose force, then? The Carnegie Battle Plan says that lesser military powers might well provide the "ground force" of 93,000 against South Africa, but that one major power might have to come in for the final showdown.

What offers, then? America? The Soviet? Britain? Who will volunteer to strike the blow for Liberalism and Free South West Africa?

Thus, companion of these pages, we come in our observation car to the coast of South West Africa and must turn our enquiring faces towards George Washington's great Republic across the sea. For there are all the answers, at the heart of the riddle inside a mystery within an enigma which America has become. We will continue, by ship or air, Americaward, where independence began with the Boston Tea Party. Where is that party now? The guns at Georgetown bear witness to the Independence which came of it. Where is that independence now? Into what hands has power passed in those United States?

... on your left, latterday pilgrims, the Statue of Liberty, then the Battery, Wall Street (there's the Woolworth Building, madam), have your custom declarations and passports ready, please ...

Here it is. Soon these United States will be two hundred years old, and where has all that led: the landings on the unknown shores of Virginia and Massachusetts, the bitter toil, the wars with the Redskins, the Westward thrust, the Civil War, the irresistible force, the insuppressible energy, the stupendous output, the gigantic wealth? Liberty or death: land of the brave and home of the free: from the halls of Montezuma to the shores of Tripolee: Monroe Doctrine: "no entanglements": what is the sum of all that now?

Sometimes I heard choirs or glee clubs of personable young men, from Harvard, Yale or elsewhere, sing a song in tones of sorrow fitted for such laments of other lands as *Over The Sea to Skye* or *Ich hatt' einen Kameraden*. The dying strain of melancholy suited the closing words, "Doomed from here to eternity".

I wondered what the American story might contain that induced this doleful foreboding in a land, greater than any other in material things, and in young men, beginning manhood, who came together to sing. After hearing the mournful number die funereally away several times I abruptly realized that these were Kipling's words, set to music. *Gentlemen Rankers Out On The Spree* was written in a South African setting a half-century before. Originally it ran:

> We're poor little lambs who've lost our way
>   Baa-baa-baa,
> We're little black sheep who've gone astray
>   Baa-baa-baa,
> Gentlemen rankers out on the spree,
> Doomed from here to eternity,
> God ha' mercy on such as we
>   Baa-baa-baa.

The words had some meaning then, though Kipling may have over-dramatized the plight of wastrel sons of lordly houses who, their heritage squandered, rode off with Somebody's Horse to the far Transvaal: they were not inevitably doomed or so pitifully in need of divine mercy, and some did well enough. Yet these words made such appeal to young America that the glee clubs took them, altered one of them ("rankers" into "songsters") and sang it so.

"Gentlemen songsters out on the spree". In that form it made no sense that I could see. Why should *songsters* be doomed from here to eternity and hope only for a forgiving beyond?

In America I often sensed this uneasy feeling about the present and future, contrasting violently with the wealth and power around, that sounded in the recurrent theme: doomed from here to eternity. Something in the songsters needed to express itself in this dolorous ballad lifted out of another time, place and context.

In three lengthy sojourns in America I felt this sub-surface apprehension, or fear of the future, more and more tangibly. I think its cause is becoming clear. It lies, in my diagnosis, in incomprehension of today's America. Americans have lost earlier beliefs because these have been taken from them; they have no clear sense of purpose because none is now to be discerned. American State policy, as declared, is to maintain America as a citadel of "the free world" against the further inroad of the destructive revolution, bent on obliterating race, nationhood, familyhood and religion. American State actions, since 1917, have progressively promoted the spread of that revolution. No adult American can remain blind to this contradiction between word and deed. Two stricken Presidents, each re-elected on the promise of peace, brought America at once into world wars, which in the sequel after victory increased the area and power of the revolution.

The twenty years following the Second War have seen the continuance of this. America makes local forays "against Communism" which leave no dent in the thing itself and end in semi-fiasco (witness Korea, Vietnam, Cuba). Betweenwhiles, American State patronage of the revolution in reality goes on and is plainest to see in Africa, where implacable American pressure for "black majority rule" has helped bring about the present chaos of racial and tribal warfare in northern Africa, under cover of which communism, leaping over the Middle East and the Indian Ocean, has planted its first overseas colony-in-embryo at Dar es Salaam on the East African coast, whence "news" about the rest of Africa reaches the ears of "the free world" through the B.B.C. and the Voice of America.

115

(In parenthesis, here a small but relevant digression. The "Free World" has received the communist-inspired picture of a "racial" conflict in Africa between two races, one big and black and the other small and white. The black people, however, are not of one *race*, but of many races. The war, in progress as I write, between the self-appointed president of Uganda, a Mr. Obote, and the deposed president, the Kabaka of Buganda, is a *racial* one with deep roots in African memories: Mr. Obote's followers are Nilotic and the Kabaka's Bantu. The endemic warfare in the Sudan, again, is a *racial* conflict between the northern Semites and the southern Nilots. The conflict in Kenya is also a *racial* one between President Kenyatta and his followers, who are Kikuyu, and his antagonist Mr. Odinga and his Nilotic supporters).

The policy of America, as proved by deeds, is not an American policy. It is that of the force, masquerading as "Liberalism", which has infested and infected every government of "the free world". By penetration it has gained control of all means of public per-suasion and the public masses are today, in fact, hypnotized by it: glued to their newspapers, radio and television, a wall has been put between them and truth. The general multitude has been reduced to that state of bewilderment and confusion which in the Liberal plan of action is the essential pre-condition for a final bid to clamp down World Government. In this situation American State actions (as distinct from proclaimed "policy") are as a high voltage cable severed and thrashing destructively about in the world.

The picture of the confused American mind might be found in the words of a Canadian professor who told his students that "the result of studies among United States high school students showed that more than half of those interviewed think most Americans are not capable of deciding themselves what is right or wrong." Such a beliefless condition would naturally produce a mass incapable of resisting any strong lead, to whatever purpose. I do not quote what else this statement contained because the source of such "studies" is obviously suspect and unverifiable and their effect could only be to implant the sense of helpless bewilderment in Canadian hearers, too.

That particular "result", however, may be near truth. Americans today are in fact utterly confused about their country's purpose and its relationship with the other world.

Americans, gazing into the future with rapt look, often used to

116

me the phrase, "the American dream". When I asked just what this was, they seemed unable or unwilling to define it, and were even somewhat embarrassed. I think it meant, to them, a longing for human improvement towards a time when man to man, the world o'er, should brothers be, but looking at the land around they felt that these hopes might be going agley and leaving them nought but grief and pain for promised joy.

Today the American dream, whate'er it be, looks like to become an American nightmare. The high voltage cable thrashes about. The "Boys" go away, unquestioningly and uncomprehendingly, to Korea, Vietnam and whither else. Senators, Congressmen, their spokesman at the United Nations, the Secretary General thereof, the Carnegie Planners, the listen-box and the look-box all accustom them to the notion that tomorrow they may move off, in the same apathetic confusion, towards Southern Africa. Is not Liberal the word and Force the action?

Thus America of the Pilgrims and the Pioneers as it stands, facing both ways, in the mid-sixties of our century. Doomed from here to eternity . . .? Is this dirge to be tomorrow's marching song, not Dolly Gray or We'll Be Over?

Let us continue, fellow sightseers, on our way. On your left the Central Library, turn right into 42nd Street, on your left Grand Central Station and, at the end of the street, a building somewhat in the shape of a tombstone . . .

. . . and this monstrous edifice, folks, is the haunt or habitat of the Benighted Nations, or B.N. As you know (or if you don't after reading this book you never will) the B.N. constitoots a permanent threat to world peace and is chiefly maintained, at enormous expense, by the United States and British Governments. It is untiring in its great work for war and in seeking out places where an explosive situation of peace exists, so that these areas may be brought to heel by the threat or use of force. It is indefatigable, also, in giving aid, derived mainly from the sources above-mentioned, to under-developed countries to help them develop their expenditures.

The B.N., friends and neighbours, this great experiment in the story of mankind, has grown vastly since it began, in 1945, as the corporate organization of the free world. Today it includes nearly every State in the world, from China to Peru, so that almost the entire earth is now, *ipso facto*, free and ain't that somep'n. Only a few remaining places, such as Southern Africa, now constitoot a threat to world war and the B.N. will know how to deal with those bums.

Great things from small beginnings flow, ladies and gentlemen, and the B.N. comprized only about fifty of the world's States when it was born at San Francisco in 1945. Who bore it? Ah'm glad you asked me that question, Ma'am. Well, its parent, as you might say, was Mr. Alger Hiss, anyways he was the first Secretary General, and he was privately devoted to the interest of the great Soviet Union, thus foreshadowing the spreading influence of that great country in the counsels of the B.N. as the years went by.

Today, friends, its membership includes nearly 120 countries. This increase is mainly due to the grand work, accomplished under the pressure of the B.N., of releasing the great black race of Africa from its white oppressors. As you will see from this new map of Africa, which looks like the pieces of a jigsaw puzzle chewed over by dogs, this produced nearly forty new recruits to the free world and to the B.N. These, together with other eminent members of the free world from Asia and the Middle East, are now able to command a majority for almost any proposal favoured by them, and this has firmly established the authority of the B.N. and its status as a permanent threat to world peace.

The B.N., ladies and gentlemen, has already done many doughty deeds, yes sirree. One of its most notable undertakings in the cause of world war was its famous expeditions to the far Congo, where its brown troops with a firm foot put down the rebellious acts of black ones against its authority, yessir, the B.N. surely showed them boys. No rose but has its thorn, my friends, and, regrettably, some of them new chums is tardy with their dues. But aid to them will no doubt be forthcoming from the treasuries of the West to enable them to catch up with these and develop their under-development, so that the membership of the B.N. shall not diminish nor their majority for its decisions decrease. Under-development by the people of the people for the people, to quote the Constitootion of the United States or was it the Gettysburg speech, I don't rightly remember, shall not perish from the earth.

And now, folks, follow me through these marble halls. Observe this press of busy girl secretaries, the thronged and well-stocked bar, the quiet (and empty, I see, well that's how it goes) Non-Denominational Place of Prayer, the whole grand mechanism of speeches and motions and resolutions, of amendments and counter-amendments, of minutes and interpreters and translators and printers, of delegates confabulating in corners, of telephones ringing, typewriters clacking, duplicating machines clicking, guides guiding, rubes rubbernecking, hayseeds gawking, them durn tourists touring, of black men, white men, brown men, yellow men, all brought together, here on the East River in little ole New York, beneath the roof of the great B.N., to unite and uphold the cause of permanent world you know what. This, folks, as you now have seen is Democracy in action, Democracy plus.

And now, as our time grows short, we will proceed by way of the Lincoln Tunnel and U.S. Highway 55 (unless I have forgotten my America) to Washington, a place where, according to the poet Southey, shines "a light for after times". Well, let us see about that . . .

119

... "Something is rotten in the State Department" said an American acquaintance to me in Washington in 1949. I was intent on learning what hidden power, invading the American machine of State, had diverted the use of American armed might in the Second War to produce the result in 1945. That came from the order to General Eisenhower, Supreme Commander, to hold back the Allied advance and thus let the Soviet Empire extend to middle Europe, obliterating Poland, Hungary, Rumania, Bulgaria, Czechoslovakia and the Baltic States: and the later order to General Marshall to support the Chinese communists in driving the free Chinese into the sea and setting up another Soviet Empire in mainland China.

The war to end dictatorship thus ended in the vast spread of that dictatorship on which Hitler modelled his. The world was left as a stage behind a dropped curtain, while the scenery was changed for another total war, intended to complete the destruction of nations and establish the World Dictatorship.

By 1949 the picture of what had gone on behind the American scenes was becoming clear. Several leading participants published books of revelation which (particularly Mr. Robert E. Sherwood's account of conditions in the White House, where he was one of several resident familiars) in other times would have produced enough moral indignation to sweep clean any stables.

Nothing happened and as I looked around I found (in 1949 and again in 1951–3 and 1956) only a strange quiescence. People knew but were not stirred. They were like the man who, being warned that the card-game was crooked, said he knew that, but it was the only game in town. I remarked this again, in a different context, during the Kefauver enquiry into the operations of the Crime Syndicate. Everything was brought to light, as the lid might be taken off a box of vipers, and all America watched through television. Again nothing happened and the Crime Syndicate (which today seems to be extending its groping tentacles into England) grew stronger. This Sicilian-born thing does not discernibly reach into politics, but its effect on the national morale must be lethal.

Then came the public exposures, first that of Mr. Alger Hiss by Mr. Whitaker Chambers. Both were captured by communism in youth at their universities. Twenty years later Mr. Hiss, risen to high office, was an exposed Soviet sympathizer, set in a place where he could do the maximum disservice to his country and the world. Mr. Chambers was by then a disillusioned ex-communist. Mr. Hiss was President Roosevelt's right-hand "adviser" at Yalta, where the deeds were done of which today we inherit the consequences.

Mr. Roosevelt's pictures at Yalta showed a man obviously dying. Mr. Churchill's physician, Lord Moran, in his diaries (now published), wondered "how far Roosevelt's health impaired his judgment" and led him to sign the infamous "Morgenthau Plan" for starving postwar Germany. At Yalta, the President "intervened very little in the discussions, sitting with his mouth open . . . I doubt, from what I have seen, whether he is fit for his job here . . . He has all the symptoms of hardening of the arteries of the brain in an advanced stage, so that I give him only a few months to live" (in the event, two months).

But Mr. Hiss was young and fit, and from Yalta went the orders that misshaped the world and the future. Six years earlier Mr. Chambers, horrified by the Stalin-Hitler pact of 1939, reported Mr. Hiss's espionage work to President Roosevelt and was contemptously brushed aside. More postwar years passed (during which Mr. Hiss was United Nations Secretary General at San Francisco) until at last the efforts of a few writers and Congressmen revealed the truth. Mr. Hiss, confronted with a mass of highly secret documents conveyed by him to Moscow, was tried and sentenced for perjury (he was never charged with treason or espionage).

In 1913 some eleven hours passed between the detection of Colonel Redl, who for years had sold Austria's military secrets to Russia, and his suicide with a revolver given him for the purpose. Ten years passed between the denunciation of Mr. Hiss and his conviction for perjury. Today another generation has grown up and by these mid-1960's its members, if caught, merely remark "So what" or something equivalent.

Disclosures in America, Canada and England followed quickly. The lid was blown off and the truth was there for the public masses to see, if they wished. The effect on their individual lives should also have been clear to them: the growing shadow of one more war, which would be twisted to serve the same destructive purpose. There was little public response, and during the 1950's and 1960's the

121

infestation of governments grew apace, and became more wide-spread than in the earlier generation of Mr. Hiss and Mr. Chambers. The new generation, all undeterred, built on the experience of the one before and white-anted away at the fabric of government in America and England alike.

In America, Mr. Hiss, as the exposures showed, was but one of a group of termites in and around the State Department. They too were exposed: some died or committed suicide, others went into the shadows. But others of the new generation took their places and in this must lie the explanation of American State policy since the Second War, which I have compared with the thrashings of a high-voltage cable broken loose. No manifest destiny is perceptible in it, only actions which must promote the advance of the revolution of destruction while purporting to oppose it.

In this process, the apparent inability of many Americans to grasp the nature of problems in the outer world, or to perceive conse-quences, may play a supporting part. At Yalta, for instance, Lord Moran noted "The Americans are leaving with a sense of achieve-ment, they feel they are on top of the world and that, while other conferences had been concerned with proposals of policy, Yalta has been the scene of important decisions that may influence the future of the world".

True enough, but in the directly opposite sense of what they thought. Mr. Harry Hopkins (the chief White House intimate) also about to die, "lying on his sickbed, is firmly convinced that a new Utopia has dawned . . . What is more remarkable—for Roose-velt is a sick man—the Americans around him do not seem to realise how the President has split the democracies . . . They cannot see that he is playing Stalin's game". (Lord Moran could not guess, when he made his notes, what sort of man moved among those "Americans around" or that some of them were privily committed to play "Stalin's game".)

"A new Utopia", thought the dying Mr. Hopkins. Then let us look at the world today, when America has announced its intention of creating another Utopia, in Africa . . .

122

. . . and therefore, good reader, we will gaze at Africa through the wrong end of the telescope, that is, from Washington, where we have now arrived, and consider the chances of this new American dream becoming a reality.

To Americans, when I came to know them, Africa was but a name, and South Africa and Rhodesia barely that. Any "national interest" of America in embroiling itself in Africa, then peaceful and improving, could not be imagined. "No entanglements" was still a remembered tenet, despite the two wars, and if new entanglements were yet to come, Africa was the last of the continents whither Americans would have expected to be dragged by them.

I first realized in 1949 that America was to become involved in Africa, and as I lived there, and had seen the effects of Utopia-making in Europe, misgiving filled me. President Truman then announced a programme for saving the world from communism. It contained a "Fourth Point" related to "undeveloped areas". It was to "foster capital investment" in them, "greatly increase the industrial activity in other nations" and "raise substantially their standards of living". Later in the year this project proved to be aimed at Africa.

Britain and other "colonial powers" were invited to co-operate in "a new defence master-plan to open up Africa south of the Sahara". Under this "huge project" new roads and railways would be built between the African possessions of Britain and those of other countries, new air bases established and scores of ports modernized." Evidently a blueprint of stupendous developments in Africa was in preparation, and Congress would need to vote great sums.

Wondering whence came this sudden interest in Africa, I did some research. The only earlier source of similar ideas that I could find was a communist book publishing during Mr. Roosevelt's period by the then American communist leader, a Mr. Earl Browder. Its proposals bore great resemblance to those evolving under Point Four: "America can underwrite a gigantic program for the industrialization of Africa . . . it must initiate a general and steady rise in the standard of life of the African peoples . . . Our government can create a series of giant industrial development corporations, each in partnership with some other government or group of governments, and set them to work upon large-scale plans of rail-road and highway building, agricultural and industrial development, and all-round modernization in . . . the undeveloped areas of the world."

Here were two minds with a single thought, the one in Moscow the other in Washington. Without being grossly cynical, I reasoned that Mr. Browder's heart beat for the world revolution, not for the African peoples. Here, it seemed, was the original blueprint of the Point Four blueprint for Africa, and someone must have sold it as an original to somebody in Washington, as dealers have occasionally been known to pass off a bogus painting as a genuine Old Master.

Mr. Browder's proposals, in any event, were essentially the same as President Truman's, so that, once again, the aims of American policy and of communism were not opposites, but the same, and this time they converged, as the prongs of the pincers, in Africa. Everything that has happened in Africa since 1949 shows this pincer method at work. When Britain attacked Egypt in 1956 (a mistake in my opinion: but once begun, 'twere best carried through) America and Russia joined to stop the operation. After that Suez fiasco came the deluge in Africa, with America ever pressing for "black majority rule" and communism creeping into the vacuum thus left, arming terrorists and esconcing itself at Dar es Salaam.

The event of 1949 seemed to me to show that, although Mr. Hiss was gone, infiltration of the American governmental machine went on, as the new generation stepped into the preceding one's shoes. President Truman, a staunch man, evidently believed that this project would in fact help produce a new Utopia, armoured against communism, in Africa. He was new to world machinations, knew Africa not, and was wrong.

The Fourth Point took clearer shape as the years passed. Officials, bureaus and money were needed for it, and a report from Washington announced that these new-age officials were working to the principle of "a new type of benevolent imperialism, designed to spread prosperity without exacerbating political nationalism". (In time the exacerbation of what came to be called "African nationalism" proved to be the chief effect). Then, "American nationals will serve *on the governmental* as well as the technical level in the politically independent countries concerned" (my italics).

124

This notion of politically independent countries governed by nationals from elsewhere seemed novel at the time but passed without comment. Up to this point, gentle reader, I have briefly summarized what I wrote seventeen years ago, when the name, Africa, had not even impinged on the mass mind. In the intervening years, when I turned to other things, I forgot much of what I earlier wrote, and was agreeably surprised when a good friend in Rhodesia, realizing this forgetfulness, induced me to read an old book of mine. I found that I had accurately diagnosed the course of events and the present shape of them, seventeen years ago.

From this point, then, I take up the story of the great defence master plan against communism in Africa, as it has developed since I wrote in 1949.

In following years a whole crop of nominally private bodies sprang up in Washington around the Africa programme. They proliferated like toadstools after rain, and like the gentle rain from heaven much monies dropped on them from the Carnegie, Rockefeller and Ford Foundations. The only admittedly official one, nesting within the government, was the African Affairs Bureau of the State Department, which, as I earlier mentioned, began to carry on a running feud with its titular superiors of the State Department in the matter of "more Liberal policies" towards Southern Africa. I cannot find whether this department earlier existed or was itself a growth of Point Four, but it developed prodigious energy in the matter of applying "pressures" in Africa.

Outside the official building, but so interlocked with it through past members of it that none could discern just where policy ended and politics began, was, above all, the Council for Foreign Relations. This, again through interlocking memberships, identified itself with the Carnegie Battle Plan in 1965. Many other groups mushroomed up and joined in the hue and cry of havoc against Southern Africa. A prominent one was the African-American Institute of New York, also closely interlocked with the others, and this produced, on behalf of the whole mass, the "United States-South African Leader Exchange Program" of 1958, which was in effect the first bid to effect in practice the appearance of "American nationals" at "governmental levels in politically independent countries" (see above).

At American universities new faculties, called "Centres of African

125

Studies" then began to appear. Several of these were conducted by former State Department officials and members of the Council on Foreign Relations, and two of them contributed to the Carnegie Battle Plan of 1965.

Supporting these central bodies in the wider field of mass agitation were numerous groups of the most varied pretensions, ranging from the Non-Denominational Crusade for Free Africa to the Crapshooters for African Democracy (these are not the true names, gentle reader, but you will get the idea). Any who wish to acquaint themselves with the ways in which "pressure" is brought to bear on governments in our day will find much information in *The Puppeteers*, by Messrs. Harold Soref and Ian Greig (1965). This shows the English counterparts of the American rabble-rousers at work and presents a lively picture of cambric'd clerics, infuriate intellectuals, bellicose Liberals, pamphleteers, poets, actresses and the rest, all clamouring for action against the white man in Southern Africa, six thousand miles away.

Most of these folk are the "useful fools" mentioned by the Venezuelan communist leader, German Lairet, in the following passage: "Through front organizations and useful fools we must demand the release of communist prisoners, howl for freedom of the press, if a communist newspaper is suppressed . . ." Our old friend Georgi Dimitroff of the Reichstag Fire Trial (he appeared in the first book I ever wrote) when he became Secretary general of the Communist International, also referred to these useful but non-initiated servitors of communism: "As Soviet power grows there will be a great aversion to Communist parties everywhere. So we must practise the techniques of withdrawal. Never appear in the foreground: let our friends do the work. We must always remember that one sympathizer is generally worth more than a dozen militant communists. A university professor who, without being a party member, lends himself to the interest of the Soviet Union, is worth more than a hundred men with party cards".

The attentive student who reads *The Puppeteers* or American publications on the same subject will usually find, low down in the list of members, patrons, sponsors, sympathizers and supporters the unobtrusive name of the fully-trained communist organizer.

These groups, in America and England, are able at any moment to produce a picket line, a little riot outside an embassy, a mass-meeting in Trafalgar Square or Madison Garden, speeches by Congressmen and M.P.'s, slanted paragraphs in the newspapers and broadcasts, Negro demonstrations, petitions to the United Nations, delegations to Washington and Westminster.

Expenditure was prodigious under President Kennedy's improvement on Point Four, when he created the Agency for International Development (A.I.D.). This, yet another new body, rests (according to its Fact Book) on the theory that "the future of a schoolboy in the United States may well depend on whether an African lad sits at a desk in a classroom or is forced to live out his life as an uneducated pawn of the power-hungry", a massive theorem which Euclid might require to be demonstrated. Among the principles governing its gifts are that the recipient country must show "social progress" (chiefly defined as "land reform"), "forego luxuries" and "accept sacrifice and discipline". A.I.D. experts and technicians are to help them towards these ends (ultimately, one supposes, at "governmental levels").

The gifts are lavish but "about 80 percent of current funds for grants and nearly 100 percent of the funds for commodities are spent in the United States". This presumably means that some of America's surplus output is sent to these recipients, who make a book entry, while the American supplier gets governmentally paid. In 1953 about 70 per cent of the expenditure of some six billion dollars went to finance the Korean war, a different form of A.I.D. Another function of A.I.D. is "to maintain access for U.S. military bases on other nations' soil".

Fear the Greeks when they come bearing gifts? If any doubt remained about American intentions towards Africa it was removed in the 1960's when President Kennedy appointed a Mr. Mennen Williams Assistant Secretary for African Affairs and sent him to Africa. At that point "African affairs" became an official activity of the American Government. Here was the President's own representative, roaming round Africa.

This might be the oddest diplomatic appointment ever made. Mr. Williams expressed open hostility to the governments in Southern Africa. Once he was smitten on the nose by an enraged white man, I believe in Rhodesia. He took no apparent umbrage and went his way, unrepentant and vocal. After some years he was seen on television, talking about "bringing down the South African

127

Government". Even Dr. Verwoerd's renowned patience then gave out and at his remonstrance Mr. Williams's resignation was accepted by President Johnson who "deeply regretted that we will not have your fine and steadying hand in critical assignments, which you have discharged so well and faithfully". This was at least a way of putting it. Mr. Williams retired to stand for Senator in Michigan (where an unorthodox American citizen undertook to raise a fund for a memorial to the man who smote the Williams nose).

His resignation could not change the now visible fact. America was deeply involved in the African turmoil, which by the time of his disappearance enveloped all northern Africa, and was demonstrably intent on spreading its area. The United States Ambassador at the United Nations continued to mouth menaces at Southern Africa and its Secretary General on television demanded a blockade of South Africa, a demand which the reader may compare with the Carnegie Battle Plan.

Even in a mad world nothing like this was ever seen. The Secretary General of the body in New York should be at the most a rapporteur or impartial recorder, authorized to effect actions decided, not to decide actions. In the nightmare atmosphere of East 42nd Street, this little man from Burma already felt himself in command of world events.

By 1966 nothing remained of the great master defence plan against communism of 1949, or of the great undertakings originally pro-projected under Point Four. The railroads, irrigation projects, modernized ports and the rest had not materialized. All that came out of the seventeen years was a political agitation aimed against Southern Africa, where the mass of white folk live, and chaos in northern Africa. Out of that, again, came the blockade of Rhodesia, the threat of blockade against South Africa, and the menace of actual invasion.

No Utopia, then. Instead, the great American Republic teetered on the brink of ruinous courses, drawn thither by the invisible power that has propelled it in this direction, since the start of the century, with increasing momentum. It was tied, like the London government, to a destructive dogma.

In the time when national interest governed American affairs of State, a president, by name Lincoln, said in 1858: "There is a

128

physical difference between the White and Black race which I believe will forever forbid the two races living together on terms of social and political equality."

That truth of 1858 is the truth of 1966. The two races can only live, in peace, *separately*, and then on terms of social and political equality.

In 1966 another president, Mr. Lyndon Johnson, announced (while talks for a settlement went on in London) that "legitimate government" must be restored in Rhodesia and only then could steps be taken to "open the full power and responsibility of nationhood to all the people of Rhodesia, not just six percent". He added, "The foreign policy of the United States is rooted in its life at home. We will not permit human rights to be restricted in our own country and we will not support policies abroad which are based on the rule of minorities or the discredited notion that men are unequal before the law".

President Johnson must have observed by that time how greatly "human rights" have been reduced in all of northern Africa since America began its pressures there. Bloodshed and tommy-gunned minority rule are everywhere there. Even as he spoke one more new State, Uganda, fell into the spreading chaos; the Prime Minister there deposed the President, and the gunman régime took over on the ruins of one more Westminster-and-Washington-style paper constitution.

Armed minorities had grasped power at gunpoint in one "emergent" State after another in northern Africa, and more were yet to follow. In these circumstances, plain to all, the American President and men around him continued (as in the words just quoted) to address public remonstrances to the only remaining area, Southern Africa, where parliamentary government survived and where men who believed themselves wronged could appeal to that "law" which was disappearing everywhere else in Africa.*

Against the background of carnage in the rest of Africa (where the numbers of people indiscriminately slaughtered in the last few

---

*The powers of detention sparingly used in South Africa and Rhodesia against acts committed by communist-trained terrorists and saboteurs from outside are exceptional ones employed by many, if not most governments in the world at one time or another against violent outrages, and do not justify the charge that men in these countries are "unequal before the law". The point is that in northern Africa there *is* now no law, with local exceptions which seem likely soon to disappear.

years must by now amount to the casualty-list of a major war) such statements as that just quoted are grotesquely unreal. American presidents are honourable men and the fault must lie, not in them but in those "advisers" who have played so ominous a part in American affairs in the last two generations. Presidents today seem to be surrounded by a stockade of misinformation and misguidance and this has become plain to see in the literature emerging from the periods of Presidents Woodrow Wilson and Roosevelt, and particularly in that of infiltration during President Roosevelt's time.

President Johnson succeeds to an edifice of apparently absolute power which is demonstrably weakened at all levels below the peak by this infiltration under the cover-name of Liberalism. He finds himself in that position at what might be the most dangerous moment in all our history, and is certainly perilous to his own country.

Let us, then, gentle reader, consider The Powers Of The President . . .

THE PINNACLE OF WEAKNESS

During the last war Mr. Churchill once told the Commons, "The United States is now at the highest pinnacle of her power and fame". President Roosevelt, learning this, said, "What Winston says may be true at the moment, but I'd hate to say it, because we may be heading before very long for the pinnacle of our weakness".

Whatever he may have meant, the ominous words remain. The weakness was already there; its source lay in the infestation of the circles around him and the way in which others used his, apparently absolute power. The "Fireside Chats" gave America the Big Daddy image (and today television is infinitely more potent in projecting this vision into a myriad homes). The forces around and behind a President are not seen.

None of the presidents in whom increasing power came to be vested in truth wielded it. President Wilson was the captive of men around him, as those who study Colonel House's *Papers* and strange novel, *Philip Dru*, may see. Congress applied the checkrein to President Wilson after the First War and that might be the last time that Congress proved able to curb a president. After that, in President Roosevelt's twelve years, the presidential power grew and grew until, during the Second War Mr. Anthony Eden, concerned about various territorial rearrangements which President Roosevelt had suggested to the Soviet's M. Molotoff, enquired in Washington about the President's constitutional authority for reshaping the globe. Mr. Berle, then Assistant Secretary of State, was consulted and replied that the President could do anything he liked "without any Congressional action in the first instance" and "the handling of the military forces of the United States could be so managed as to foster any purpose he pursued".

Managed! That was in war, and who *wielded* this power and *managed* the purpose. A strange family of familiars and intimates inhabited the White House then, and some were spiritual kindred of the agents of revolution who had crept into the State Department. The chief one, a Mr. Harry Hopkins, was described to me by Americans as a "smalltime fixer" and "little brother of the rich". The appearance of such a man at the peak of American affairs at so dangerous a moment must be something unique in any history.

131

His biographer, Mr. Robert E. Sherwood (also an inmate of the White House) says of him that until the war's end (which was also his and the dying President's end) he was in decisive matters "the de facto President", yet he had "no legitimate official position nor even any desk of his own except a card table in his bedroom".

Mr. Hopkins in fact wielded the world power vested in the President. He was given charge of the distribution of treasure, munitions and supplies under the Lease Lend bill, and diverted the bulk of it, unknown to the public masses, to the Soviet Union. If any copies of Major Racey Jordan's *Diaries* have survived the literary terror, readers may in them study this, the most stupendous transfer of wealth from one country to another ever known; and all done, in his own unfettered right and discretion, by "Harry the Hop".

Being irritated by suggestions that the Soviet should provide information about its military situation, as did the British, before further supplies were sent, Mr. Hopkins decreed:

"The United States is doing things which it would not do for other United Nations without full information from them . . . There is no reservation about the policy at the present time but the policy is constantly being brought up by various groups for rediscussion. I propose that no further consideration be given to these requests for rediscussion".

Here is imperial power in action, wielded by a Mr. Hopkins. He resumed, on a much vaster scale, the policy begun by the men around President Wilson, who in 1917 spoke of "the wonderful and heartening things that have been happening in the last few weeks in Russia" and the next day granted the provisional government there credits amounting to $325,000,000. The hammer-and-anvil process, by means of which the revolution in Asia and high finance in America, while grimacing at each other as if at daggers drawn, in fact combined to beat the world into a flaccid mass ready to receive the iron imprint of World Government, was thus continued.

Mr. Sherwood, an adoring habitué of the White House in war, when he looked back later was deeply concerned by what he saw with a soberer eye. He then developed an "alarmed awareness of the risks that we run of disastrous fallibility at the very top of our Constitutional structure". There was "far too great a gap between the President and Congress", he decided, and noted that "the

132

extraordinary and solitary constitutional powers of the President remain and, in times of crisis, they are going to be asserted for better or for worse".

Today "the gap" has even widened. The President can do what he will, for better or worse. We live in a time of permanent, though engineered crisis. An eminent authority who perceived the mortal danger long before Mr. Sherwood's illusions faded, Dr. Charles A. Beard (in *President Roosevelt and the Coming of the War*, 1941) said:

"At this point in its history, the American Republic has arrived under the theory that the President of the United States possesses limitless authority publicly to misrepresent and secretly to control foreign policy, foreign affairs, and the war power." Dr. Beard saw the period in which we now move as "the supreme test of American statesmanship" and feared the future because there was now "no divinity hedging our Republic against Caesar".

Such are the legacy, the post and the power bequeathed to President Johnson (by the accident of another's assassination). Texan politics are a far cry from the realities of world events and one must wonder if he perceives the true shape of his time. His words, quoted at the end of the previous chapter, are of ill omen in that respect.

He has on his hands at the moment a war in Vietnam which, like the Korean one, seems to be of those new-age wars which must not be won. For that reason it is unpopular in America. Nevertheless, he has been reported as saying that whenever he makes peace moves his popularity rating goes down. Here is another example of the dangerous influences around a President, who must be guided by national interest above any other. None can know how or by whom these "public opinion polls" are operated, but they are evidently made use of by the "advisers" who nowadays surround American presidents.

About the same time the President proposed to the Kremlin that the Moon be not used for military purposes and that other planets be peacefully explored. A draft treaty to ensure this happy consummation, the reports added, was to be laid before the United Nations. (At this point I was disabled for a while from work on this book, suffering from prostration following an attack of hysterical laughter.)

The President has matters to think on here in Earth before he

133

glances Moonward. His governmental machine, by all the signs, is still permeated by agents of the revolution, and a great uproar of "witch-hunt" goes up at any attempt to winkle them out. Around them, again, is the clamorous mass of "Liberal" bodies, all crying for "force". At the United Nations, African politicos with one-man-one-gun dictatorships behind them, scream (I use the word literally) for an American-British war against Southern Africa.

On his pinnacle of weakness stands today's American President, immune from Congressional guidance and control, hemmed in by "advisers". A terrible responsibility rests on the one man in the world who can, alone, unleash another total war. Between it and him, in fact, lies only a four-letter word: veto. The greatest of the pressures brought to bear on him is to prevent him ever using it.

Our century has seen that the power vested in American presidents has become absolute, but in the recent past has been wielded by others. Then what do these others want, to what ultimate purpose do they use any power they can exert?

Here, at last, we come to the very root of the matter, and of evil, good friends. This way please, to a place as dark, sinister, tortuous and intricate as the Labyrinth of Hawara or the catacombs of Rome: to the world of WAPWAG . . .

FOR YOUR FRIENDS

Your relatives and friends overseas are eager to know the truth about Rhodesia and South Africa. Send them *The Battle for Rhodesia!* Do that today. If you have any difficulty in getting copies locally use the coupon below.

HAUM
P.O. Box 1371
CAPE TOWN, South Africa

Please send me..............................copies of T H E BATTLE FOR RHODESIA by Douglas Reed at R1.85 (18/6) per copy.
I enclose the amount of................ ....
(Postage extra: 5c locally, 12c overseas.)

NAME ....

ADDRESS ....

....

....

(If you want copies to be sent direct to your friends, write their names and addresses below or on the reverse side of this page.)

9240/637 ⚜ Citp.

In this century we have seen empires and kingdoms, monarchs and princes, presidents and republics crumble and go. Each step was supposed to lead to something "new" and better, and each was followed by deterioration. No pattern of improvement, of a rising brotherhood of man, emerged from it all. The only pattern, if such it can be called, was that of destroying old things without putting better ones in their place: witness the world today.

However, one discernible *thread* ran through the disorderly process. It was that of world revolution leading to despotic world government. For this reason the process could not stop, any more than a stone rolling downhill. It had to come to fruition or finally fail, and this moment of decision now bears down on us all.

Students much more erudite than I, who have examined this matter, find that their search takes them into olden times, indeed, into ancient ones. Let us here take it up at the point where it became visible in our recent world, and carry the story, briefly, through to this day.

It all began then, for our purpose, with the chance discovery (as accidental as that of Mr. Whitaker Chamber's Hiss-incriminating "pumpkin papers") by the Royal Bavarian Government in 1787 of the documents of a secret society, the Illuminati of Adam Weishaupt, a university professor. Obviously this plan for world revolution (the papers can be read by any who care to undertake the research) cannot have sprung, as by demoniac birth, from the mind of one man: a long history of organisation and conspiracy clearly preceded it.

However, these documents for the first time proved the existence of the revolutionary conspiracy which we know today as communism (it has had various other names). It is identifiable from them as the same thing, for all the aims and methods are there: the cell system of organization (only when the papers were published did most of the Illuminates know that Weishaupt existed or was the head): the use of aliases (cover names); the employment of "useful fools" (high clerics and princes, believing themselves to be of "Liberal" mind, were among its members, and a Duke of Brunswick, when he saw the real aims, made anguished confession of his

135

duplicity); the denunciation of parents; the use of ciphers, poisons and explosives; and all the rest. The aims were the eradication of religion, family, nations and the establishment of world government.

The Illuminati played a large part in the secret societies behind the French Revolution and then extended their influence to America, so that George Washington expressed himself "fully satisfied that the doctrines of the Illuminati have spread to the United States". They were exposed by three writers, Messrs. Barruel, Robison and Morse and one of George Washington's last acts was to thank Mr. Morse for his work, "the dissemination of which would be useful, if spread through the community" (Mr. Whitaker Chambers, in 1939, received a presidential recommendation to "go jump in the lake" when he offered his revelations). I was surprised to find how far control of the press in America had gone even in that time: Messrs. Barruel, Robison and Morse were "smeared" out of literary existence.

The revolutionary conspiracy then went underground for a time and after Napoleon's fall emerged behind a Christian cover-name, calling itself The Holy Alliance. It was perceived to be an attempt at a supernational dictatorship and that name faded out, but the subversive work continued and appeared in France again towards the mid-century under one Louis Blanc, who worked for "World Revolution" and the super-State.

Probably few people in Texas, even today, ever heard of Louis Blanc, but thirty years later still a young Texan, one Edward Mandell House, was absorbing ideas "reminiscent of Louis Blanc and the revolutionaries of 1948" (the editor of his *Papers*).

This "Colonel" House, when the new century broke, became one of the group of men who chose a little-known university professor, one Woodrow Wilson, to be candidate for the Presidency. Mr. House boasted (his *Papers*) that he infused ideas into other men's minds; the ideas, as has been seen, were those of Louis Blanc.

At that time Mr. House's "ideas" about the total shape of the grand conspiracy were limited. The hero of his novel of 1912 (when Mr. Wilson became president) was an American dictator who wished to bring about "an international grouping or league of powers founded on Anglo-Saxon solidarity" (a very different thing

136

from what later developed). Nevertheless, the central idea was there: some body *above nations**.

Mr. House was virtually president during Mr. Wilson's two terms (the *Papers*) and thus wielded the presidential power. He discussed the great "idea" with the ailing British Foreign Minister, Sir Edward Grey, and the shape of it changed again. The two men now talked about some super-national body that should combine against States which committed inhumane acts in war. The central idea continued: some authority *over nations*. Sir Edward fell into the trap and then proposed "some league of nations *backed by force*". Later Sir Edward, with the familiar Liberal dislike of words revealing intention, backed away from "force" and substituted the genteel-sounding "sanctions".

But not for long. In 1916 Mr. House prompted President Wilson publicly to support the plan for "some league of nations" before a body then newly-formed: The League To *Enforce* Peace. Thus the Plan became clearer: peace was to be enforced by war. Lord Robert Cecil demurred at that point, reminding Mr. House that the Holy Alliance too began as "a league to enforce peace" but in fact became "a league to uphold tyranny" (today's demonstrable concept).

Then Mr. House set up a body called "The Inquiry" to draft the plan of "a new world order". The drafters were three little-known persons: a Dr. Sidney Mezes (Mr. House's brother-in-law), a Dr. Isaiah Bowman, and a Mr. Walter Lippman,(whom I believe to be still with us). In all this President Wilson played no part beyond giving his public blessing to The League To Enforce Peace: Mr. House says that the President "never seriously studied" the matter and was not the author of the League of Nations, with which the First War ended. Nevertheless, the obedient Mr. Wilson then insisted on a new "general association of nations", so that, out of all the earlier spadework behind the scenes, came the League of Nations of 1919.

That League collapsed in 1939 and throughout the Second War

---

*Philip Dru is unreadable as fiction but politically and historically of major interest. Mr. House shows in it the process of picking a man to be used by others as their instrument when in power. It also contains a remarkable disclosure: that mechanical eavesdropping (known as "bugging" in our day: a device whereby such men may gain a "hold" over their chosen victim) was known in 1912, or earlier! I fancy that Mr. House's motive in writing this strange book may have been to hint to others in the group that he "knew something" about them which could be used if they were to "rat" on him.

the leading men of the West continued, as if possessed, to declare that the creation of another super-national body must be a foremost aim of victory. During that war the grand design was unremittingly pursued and again persons behind the scenes proved in the event to know more about the outcome than presidents, prime ministers and the public masses.

For instance, a Mr. Moritz Gomberg was presumably unknown to the multitudes embroiled when in 1942 he popped up with a "Group for a New World Order" and published a map showing the re-arrangement of the globe. He foresaw that at the war's end the communist empire would extend from the Pacific to the Rhine (Berlin is not far from the Rhine), that a Hebrew State should be set up in Palestine (which happened), that the remnant of Western Europe should disappear in a "United States of Europe" (something which is now being actively pursued), and that the African continent should become a "Union of Republics" (it is becoming a shambles, the same thing).

Mr. Churchill then seems to have become aware that all was not going as he thought the war's purpose to be, and remonstrated: "Let me make this clear, in case there should be any mistake about it in any quarter. We mean to hold our own. I have not become the King's First Minister in order to preside over the liquidation of the British Empire . . . Here we are and here we stand, a veritable rock of salvation in this drifting world". (His then son-in-law, twenty years later, said "We have lost the will to govern", according to Sir Roy Welensky).

The war ended. The United Nations was ushered into being by Mr. Alger Hiss and twenty years have shown what it has done and yet might do. By 1953 the One-Worlders, waiting for the sunrise, evidently thought that the great day was at hand, and also the instrument, the United Nations.

In that year the full shape of the Grand Design, the Master Plan, at length emerged. This, in our current idiom, was It. In this document the world might see just what awaited it, if all the "ideas" took shape. Here is no longer any vague talk of some league to enforce something. Here is the Grand Design worked out in detail, so that any man can see just how it would affect him, his family, his future and his world. This is the plan which, in my estimation, our One-Worlders aspire to carry through under cover of another war, if

138

the American president of the day can be prevented from saying: "Veto".

It came from a body calling itself The World Association of Parliamentarians for World Government, or WAPWG. To make this unutterable hieroglyph utterable, I will borrow a vowel and call it henceforth WAPWAG. It is, or was, but one of the unnumerable "front" bodies working towards the revolutionary end. However, this one produced, at its second conference in 1952, the Master Plan. It deserves a chapter to itself.

Come, gentle reader, and consider Wapwag's Master Plan for the world . . .

The Wapwag, conference of 1952, then, found before it a blueprint of "The World Organization". This, said the document, "will take over the existing facilities of the United Nations". That being done, The World organization would set up a directorate composed of A World Director; eight Zone Directors; five Commanders; and fifty-one Regional Directors. The World Organization's charter would "effect World Security so that the people of the World may live in freedom from fear of war" (for which purpose substantial land,sea and air forces would be stationed around the globe). It would control the production and distribution of basic foodstuffs, raw and strategic materials, and allow Governments "the maximum freedom of action within the understanding of World achievement".

So much for the broad outline of this global rearrangement. Next, the details:

All these high world officials would be nominated, subject to the approval of The World Director, by the governments designated. As to the super-despot, The World Director, that is the only blank in the plan. By whom *he* is to be nominated or appointed, is not stated, so presumably He (or She) will appoint himself or herself. As He, or She, is to rule The World, the method of selection, or self-election, might be of universal interest, but that point is left open.

Beneath Him, or Her, the eight Zone Directors would administer the globe, each at some place far distant from his native land. The Swedish Government, for instance would appoint the Director of the Australian Zone, with headquarters in Sydney. The Chinese Government would nominate the Director of the African Zone, headquartered at Khartoum. France would send the South American Zone Director to Rio, England supply the Polar one (based on London), India the European Director at Paris, the Soviet the Zone Director for North America, who would dwell in Chicago, the American Government would supply the Zone Director for India, at Delhi, and South Africa would provide a Zone Director, resident at Shanghai, for China.

This is what an English North Country comedian would call "a proper mook-oop", but it is seriously intended, witness the high

140

personages who adorned Wapwag. They were mostly of the Liberal kind who can be plucked from the trees of credulity and vanity like nuts in the fall. They were originally supposed all to be "parliamentarians", but this qualification was widened to include "former members of parliament", which in our times would let in all sorts and conditions of men. The membership of Wapwag contained many persons of the kind mentioned by Georgi Dimitroff as lending themselves to the interest of the Soviet Union without being party-members and being "worth more than a hundred men with party cards". In the lower echelons the figures of a few true initiates could be perceived.

The fifty-one Regional Directors, subordinated to the five Zone Directors who would be subordinate to the One World Director, would similarly be distributed around the world on the far-from-home pattern. A female Soviet citizen, for instance, would administer the Desert Region from Goa, and a Finnish woman the Congo from Brazzaville; a Brazilian woman would rule the Balkans from Belgrade and a Danish one Central Europe from Prague. Liberia would supply Scandinavia with a Regional Director, based on Stockholm, and Holland a Dutch one for Egypt, posted at Cairo; and so on round the earth.

All this would rest on a rearrangement of the world's armed forces, which would come forthwith under The World Director. They would be combined in a World Security System under five Commanders: the World Security Commander, the Air Security Commander, the Sea Security Commander, the Untersee Commander, and the Research and Development Commander. A point that caught my curious eye in this list was that of "Untersee Commander". The Plan is couched in English throughout save for this one term: Untersee Commander, used in apparent preference to "submarine" or "underwater". Probably some significance lies in this particular choice of a word, with its memories of the dreaded "U-Boats", but I cannot divine what it may be.

All ground armies of the world would come under the Land Director, and would be used in the following proportions and places. The Soviet would supply four garrison and two field divisions to be stationed at Mobile in the U.S.A., Dar es Salaam, Madras, Shanghai, Australia and Canada. The United States would supply an equal number to Argentina, Bulgaria, Czechoslovakia, India, and Australia. The remaining white members of the British Commonwealth, Britain, Eire, Canada, Australia, and New Zealand would provide six divisions for China, the United States, Russia and Latvia.

In this way a total of forty-nine garrison and nine field divisions would be distributed as forlorn foreign legions throughout the world, the only essential being that they should be fed up and far from home, and the further the better. Any land forces remaining after this rearrangement would be disbanded and "absorbed into industry and agriculture".

As to naval and merchant forces, all vessels, personnel "and equipment whatsoever of national, union or commonwealth sea forces would be reallocated as required by the Commander Sea Security". Any surplus "would be disposed of under orders issuing from the World Organization". Sea bases would be handed over to it "if necessary, on lease from the owner nation".

Similarly in the domain of the Commander Air Security: all aircraft, airfields and personnel would be incorporated within the World Organization scheme for air security and come under his command. The Commander Untersee would take over all underwater craft "and paraphernalia whatsoever", use what he wanted "and dispose of the remainder". The Research and Development Commander would take over "all scientific research establishments".

Service in this World Security Force would be by "professionals", that is, conscripts, who would serve for between fifteen and twenty-two years. All petroleum, metals and commodities usually designated as strategic materials, and shipping completed and at sea would come under the World Organization, which "operates in the acknowledgement that a world system is necessary". All trade agreements between governments, and their plans for future development of basic needs, would be coordinated by the World Organization, which would maintain "the World Account" (in "World Marks").

So there it is, the last word in World Planning. I hope not to have prompted derision by this summary, for it is to be taken seriously: how far have we not already been brought in this direction, behind the smokescreen of two world wars?

I do not know if Wapwag exists today. Whether or not is no matter, because a vast complex of kindred groups and bodies carries on the work, and they have had much success in furthering it to this stage. I had the impression when I first drew attention to this Master Plan (in 1953) that it might have erred in letting a copy or two out of the bag. Anyway, I was much vilified at the time for the modest public reference I made to it.

Postscript: I said, above, that the Master Plan was the last word, to which nothing could be added to make intention clearer, and once again I was wrong. As I write, perspiring reader, I learn that our One-Worlders already have extended their plan to the very Cosmos.

In 1966, after President Johnson proposed a treaty to prevent the Moon being used for military purposes and for the peaceful exploration of other planets, I foresaw the day when, the Moon having been colonized and settled by valiant pioneers, our One-Worlders would surge thither in their footsteps, crying One Moon and Moon Government, so that the whole business would begin again up there.

Sure enough, a few days later The Committee to Study the Organization of Peace, (COMSOP), recommended that the United Nations should take over ownership of the high seas and outer space. Seventy "scholars, writers, editors, union leaders and business executives" signed this report, which urged that the General Assembly of the United Nations should "declare the title of the international community" to the high seas and outer space.

WAPWAG first, and now COMSOP. Angels and ministers of grace . . .

. . . and now that we have journeyed together half round the world, and seen how the mechanism of power-politics is operated, let us return by air to the place where all this began: Rhodesia; and look at the world again from there.

Even the ancient truisms are being exploded in this, the century of destiny, among them the one that there is nothing new under the sun. Man's conquest of space *is* something new. Even in our time that was but an eccentric's fantasy, and now it is happening. Soon no mysteries will remain save that of life itself, and its meaning.

Man is about to move into space and to other worlds. He has no choice about that, for he is over-populating his Earth. This century is the period of the great acceleration, in all human things. A small span of years has carried man from his first power-driven flights to the recoil-propelled capsule in which he seeks the stars. This same, sudden acceleration, as if a foot were abruptly pressed hard down on a pedal, is evident in all mortal things, and most of all in the headlong increase of population, at a rate of multiplication never before known. This is a thing of our time.

We have not reached the result which Malthus foresaw, the point where the numbers of human beings would far outrun the supply of food, and are not likely to come to that for a long time yet, because of those methods of increasing food supply which he could not envisage. The population-explosion is leading to another effect than that of mass starvation: to overcrowding. Even between two neighbours frictions arise, and the future which now is opening to Man on Earth is that of an intolerable propinquity. Man is not meant to live either alone or in a hive. Our cities grow too big and suburbanization spreads ever further into the surrounding country until the very cities begin to meet: this process is to be seen in every land known to me.

Man has to go elsewhere or ultimately perish, and precisely at this point he begins to move into Space. Thus he is not going of his own volition, but is impelled by forces beyond his ken. Sublime paradox: Man never looked more like a performing flea, controlled and directed by an uncomprehended hand, than at the moment of his greatest triumph: The Conquest Of Space!

Nevertheless, the contrast between the culminating achievement of the white race in space and its inert confusion on earth is startling. Up there in the stratosphere all is valour and striving: down here in the catastrosphere all is villainy and strife. For the nonce we can but look around and marvel at the mundane pandemonium and then look up and ask whether, when we people Space, we shall pollute it too.

For there, too, the doughty "pioneers" whom we watch today will be followed by hardy "settlers" and "colonists", and when they have made all secure, the generation of vipers, bearing the yellow flag of "Liberalism", will follow too, crying for Space Government and a Space Director. Most ominously, a Moon Peace Treaty has already been proposed (as I reported earlier), so that the Moon, now serenely shining, in course of time would also become a permanent threat to Space Peace, and the clamour for Space War, in the councils of the United Planets, may already be heard in the distance.

Considering our Earthly affairs as they look at this point in time, it might be better that we do not colonize Space at all. The wiser course, at all events, would be to tidy up matters on Earth before we go there. To use the vernacular, I recall the homely phrase of the British soldier from the wars returning around 1919, when the name "Mesopotamia" was being dinned into his ears: "Never mind about Mesopotamia: let's clear up the mess-up at 'ome 'ere".

And that brings us back again to the place where we began: Rhodesia. It is a small place in the crazy chequerwork of our world, but at this moment plays the vital part in our affairs, as the arm of the legendary Dutch boy, thrust through the hole in the dam, kept out the waters.

From here, on the sunlit roof of Africa, you get a wide, clear view of the raging, confused, tumultuous sea, so oft encarnadined, which is the outer world. Here an epic struggle, in the truest sense of the word, has been fought by a few men who, having taken the tide in the affairs of men at what may be its turn, might yet lead their country and the world to better fortunes. If they fail, worse days await us all.

Rhodesia, having earned its independence decades since, has in the past seven months (June of 1966, as I conclude this book) established and proved it. Behind that dam, clear water and safe anchorage spread over all Southern Africa, and given time and the acknowledgment of its just cause, the chaotic waters in Africa north of the Zambezi will withdraw and settle too.

The American President, in his most recent speech as I write, said that until recent times darkest Africa was not so dark as America's ignorance of it, and that, I vouch from my own experience, is a true word. He added that Africa was now seen to be "a mosaic of peoples", not one black mass clamouring unanimously for liberation, and that these peoples should be let or led to form nations in their own fashion. This is another true word, indeed, it is two-thirds of the way to the whole truth of Africa. The remaining, and most important part of truth, is that the mosaic is not an all-black, but a black and white one, in which white nations too must build their nations as they need. If that last stage in the realization of truth comes to the White House, peace will become secure again in Africa, and another total war, beginning in Africa, be averted (on more than one recent occasion the world only just skated by that danger, as a blindfold skater a hole in the ice). After that, we might with clearer conscience and better hope turn our minds to The Conquest Of Space, and its colonization.

The name "Liberal" has been identified with what has happened in Africa in the last ten years, and for that reason has come to stink in the nostrils of people who live in Africa and have understanding of, and a true feeling for the black folk among whom they live. It is repugnant to think that so much carnage has been caused in the names of "Liberal opinion", "world opinion", democracy, one-man-one-vote and other false slogans. I would like to see these good people taken to the scenes of massacre and mass graves, mutilation and indiscriminate slaughter. Tribal wars have begun again on all hands, slavery has reappeared, and in time tribes which once were cannibal will resume their ancient practice.

The worst effect, among these effects, is that of slavery resumed. White people who live in Africa do not form moral opinions about the ways of black ones, for they know how deeply rooted these are in beliefs and customs rooted in centuries beyond compute. Some of them hesitate morally to condemn even human sacrifice in such places (for instance, Basutoland) where it is part of a tribal religion, shared and accepted by the tribe. It is punished by the white man, while he rules, but wisdom and experience forbid them to cry

146

"Holier than thou", or to pass moral judgment as they execute a legal one.

But in one matter all agree. Slavery is wrong by any standard. To take the responsibility for black tribes' reversion to this trade is to assume blood guilt. Remember, good reader, that slavery was not an iniquitous thing practised solely by Arab captors and traders. It was a method of commerce practised by the warrior tribes on the weaker ones. The captives were saleable commodities and were considered as such. This was a two-way traffic of supply and demand, and the black men supplied the black victims.

When the white man came and stamped it out, slavery was already beginning to depopulate eastern and central Africa. That is one reason why only 400,000 people remained in what is now Rhodesia, where now are over four million black folk. In Africa north of the Zambezi, now that the protecting hand has been withdrawn and "pressure" from America has been used to extend the area of such "liberation", the condition is returning of which the great Arab slaver from Zanzibar, old Tippu Tib, said a hundred years ago, "The man with the gun is the king of Africa".

Once again: the white man demonstrably gave the black one life, in Africa, and when the white man goes the black folk begin again to kill, mutilate, burn, publicly hang and enslave each other. They have not had time to learn otherwise, and do not yet *wish* to change. Against the further spread of this evil stand Rhodesia, where law, order and protection in the white man's understanding of the words prevail, and its neighbours in Southern Africa.

They stand also against the menace of a third general war, which in my judgment must inevitably come out of the African shambles if England and America continue their effort to extend the area of chaos southward from the Zambezi.

Can any book avert a war? A book can *make* a war. That has been done. *Uncle Tom's Cabin* so incensed the North and embittered the South that in time the smouldering quarrel burst into the red flame of one of the most destructive wars in history.* Obviously no book or books could stop war as such, for it appears to be something

*President Lincoln, when he met Mrs. Harriet Beecher Stowe, greeted her as "the little lady who started the big war". Mrs. Beecher Stowe, when she visited the ruined South and (like Lizzie Borden) saw what she had done, would fain have lured back and cancelled out *Uncle Tom's Cabin*, or at any rate part of it, written in ignorance of reality.

inherent in human nature, as male infants begin to fight as soon as they can walk.

Just possibly, however, a book might help avert a *particular* war, another "unnecessary" one like that of 1939–45. Such was my vain hope in writing *Insanity Fair* and is my motive in writing *The Battle For Rhodesia*. I aim to show you what is truly at stake, gentle reader: to give you a little information which you will not otherwise receive, and to bring you to my way of thinking. The world has been brought near the verge of another "unnecessary" war through the situation artificially created in Africa. Now is the moment to recoil and reverse the process.

Rhodesia's is a just and good cause, and I was fortunate to be able to conclude a writer's life by watching the siege of 1965–6. Had the quiet men in Salisbury cracked, we would all have been a big step nearer the big war: tribal warfare and general chaos would be starting now in Rhodesia and the attack would have been turned, through the gap thus made, on South Africa and the Portuguese territories, with redoubled vigour. The outcome is not yet clear: the future still hangs on the razor's edge. If the Rhodesians prevail, they will have done the white man everywhere, and the world, a decisive service by resisting and turning back the destructive tide of the last fifty years.

SALISBURY, 1966

This year of disgrace, 1966, has reached the month of July and the international *opera bouffe*, with the bailiffs waiting in the wings, continues on a mounting scale.

A British Prime Minister has publicly congratulated himself on obtaining leave from the carpetbagging assembly in New York to blockade Beira and so to convert "an act of piracy into a legal act of peacemaking". Shades of Pitt and Palmerston, and of the British sea-captains who a century ago drove the slave-traders from these very waters! England's proudest boast, the freedom of the seas, falls into the waves like a struck flag on a scuttled ship.

The British Government, after blockading Rhodesia for seven months, was itself blockaded for seven weeks by its own seamen. It took "emergency powers" against this menace and its head accused the Communists (he named names) of instigating this attempt on the life of the nation. Nothing escapes Mr. Wilson's eye, as the reader will observe: and yet, in Rhodesia, he would not allow that any but the Communist-prompted terrorist parties spoke for "the people".

Would I could live to see, and chuckle over, what our learned friend, The Future Historian, will make of this time (but I think I know: I have already seen what he made of the years leading to The Second War and of its results). This present scribe is troubled to know whether to tell today's tale in terms of comedy, farce, burlesque, comedy, melodrama or tragedy. If he were not, like of all of us, involved in it, and in mankind, he would have to use the analogy of the harlequinade, for never were such double-somersaults of doubletalk, such whackings with the bladder of cant, such chases by Keystone Kops apeing true guardians of the law, such pratfalls on the banana-skin of reality, such fantastic contortions of truth, where the face of mockery, bent over backwards, peers from between the straddled legs of propaganda. However, in this panto-mime Capitano Horribilicribifax carries no cardboard sword, but a tommy-gun: the clown, no string of sausages, but grenades made to a diagram supplied from far, Asiatic workshops; and the four horsemen wait at the stage-door.

In this comedy of terrors, harlequin (if I may be forgiven the

149

word) leaped on to the African stage, waving the wand of sophistry, in the person of a young political gentleman, a Mr. Robert Kennedy, brother of a murdered president and by general assumption aspirant to the next, or next-but-one term in the White House.

I have shown the unfettered power wielded by, or at any rate used in the name of American presidents today, to the unhampered last use of which the events of the fifty years have brought them. I alluded then to the present incumbent, Mr. Lyndon Johnson. After Mr. Kennedy's leap into Africa, and the things he said here, the contemporary historian must record that the danger inherent in that state of affairs in the White House will be even greater in future.

Diplomacy is a dead thing, and the B.N. building in New York is its gravestone (prayers might well be offered in the churches for the return of "secret diplomacy" in these times when all is open and nothing is revealed). Now, even ordinary manners seem to have dropped from international usage, for when before did ever a president-presumptive, or even a responsible politician, cross the ocean to an unknown, friendly foreign country and behave as this political gentleman behaved?

Mr. Kennedy came six years after Mr. Macmillan's "wind of change" speech and thus, if he came "to learn" (as he said) could have learned of the chaos and carnage which have come on all Africa north of the Zambezi in the sequel to that speech. Instead, he made another "wind of change" speech, which to people living in Africa meant that, if history repeated itself, the area of chaotic Balkanization would be spread to the remaining, still orderly area of the continent.

He was led from meeting to meeting of university students, of an age and kind similar to those of Mr. Alger Hiss and Mr. Whitaker Chambers when they were infected by communism at their American universities forty years ago. These young, unwary, inexperienced folk can be, and are, whipped into a frenzy of excitement by anyone from a pop-singer to a politician, if the advance publicity be loud enough, and in this case they responded to the propagandist persuasion in the way to be expected.

Apart from that, Mr. Kennedy moved from group to group of "liberal intellectuals", many of whom were, by their records, demonstrably associated with the communist plan to bring about

150

outside intervention in southern Africa. These people have unhindered access to world publicity for their notions: on the rare occasions when they have come under examination by trained questioners, and have had to account for what they have said and done, they become so confused by the record that they collapse like pricked balloons (I have a notorious example in mind).

Moving in these circles, Mr. Kennedy, who knew nothing of Africa, gave no glance to the chaotic conditions in the north, outside peaceful southern Africa. After his few days here he flew blithely over Uganda (where the latest massacre was in progress: that of the Buganda tribespeople by the gunmen of the self-appointed dictator, a Mr. Obote) and landed happily at Dar es Salaam. This, as I have shown, is the Tanzanian port used for the continuous shuttle-service of outward-bound trainees and inward-bound trained terrorists, to and from Moscow, Nanking and North Korea. (This fact is known to every government in the world). Mr. Kennedy, on arrival, said there was "a special bond of friendship between the United States and Tanzania", which was due partly "to a common commitment to work for human justice and equality" (the Zanzibar part of "Tanzania" groans beneath a Revolutionary Council at this time).

Looking back on orderly South Africa, Mr. Kennedy, as was to be expected, brought out the dear old phrase about an "explosive situation". If the situation there did not change, he announced after some ten days in Africa, it could become "very explosive", not only for South Africa but also for the rest of the continent.*

The reader might now consider the background of African events over the last two decades, so that he may understand the true significance of Mr. Kennedy's observations.

President Truman's "master defence plan against communism in Africa" of 1949 has during this period changed into its opposite. None can believe today that American policy towards Africa has anything to do with its defence against communism: it is aimed against the three southern States which defend *themselves* against communism.

---

*In one speech he appeared to imply that he felt himself to be accompanied by the saints and martyrs of the Church. That, at any rate, seems a reasonable interpretation of his strange remark that "from birth to death we are surrounded by an invisible company of men who never served a lesser loyalty than the welfare of mankind".

151

Lenin's original dictum, that the colonial powers must be driven from Africa, has been half-realized: not because they were driven out, but because they abdicated in all of northern Africa after Mr. Macmillan's "wind of change" speech. That leaves the southern part. How is that to be submerged in the northern chaos, and the disintegration of the entire continent achieved?

When the South African police located and raided the secret communist headquarters at Rivonia, near Johannesburg, in 1963, several of the leaders were caught and a mass of documents found. These were put in evidence at the subsequent trial and the plan for the completion of Africa's ruination became public.

It goes into the remotest details of organization, but the main heads will suffice here. The first stage is the training of terrorists in Moscow and elsewhere, and their use, on their return, for acts of sabotage: full instruction is given them in the manufacture and use of explosives, in arson and other acts of violence.

The next stage, if terrorism is successful enough, is the organization of "guerilla fighters", in companies and squads, for actual warfare: the methods used in China and Cuba are closely studied.

None of this would ever achieve anything in stable, well-governed countries like those of southern Africa. It only succeeded in the north because the protecting hand of law and order was withdrawn. An internal "rising" (the darling notion of our bellicose Liberals) cannot happen, because the native masses, having seen what happened in the north, do not want to be massacred, burned or blown up by terrorists of their own colour.

Therefore the whole plan rests on the idea of outside intervention, and the hope is that, if this were estimated to be possible, the terrorists might cause enough internal trouble for the propagandist machine in London and New York to announce that the "explosive situation" had arrived, which liberals everywhere foretell. The communist plan, which tallies exactly with the Carnegie Battle Plan published in New York, envisages a two-phase development. First, a blockade of South Africa, during which the terrorists in the country would be ordered to do as much damage as they could: the second, actual invasion on the pretence that the "explosive situation" demanded it. (The blockade of Rhodesia and the threats of "force" which have been used show how near to reality this, once unthinkable thing might be.) In the final analysis the communist plan could only succeed through such an actual armed invasion by a foreign power or powers, masquerading as a "United Nations" peace expedition on the Congo model.

The reader who has toiled through these pages has seen that over years a political mechanism was built to produce a war-situation at a given moment, that of the decision in the South West Africa matter. Here was no "drift to war" but a process engineered as by high precision tooling, and 1966, I judge, was the appointed year.

A glance at the map of Africa will show how the process was engineered to reach this point. In 1960 Africa was a continent of order. By 1966 Africa north of the Zambezi was an area of chaotic disorder. To show himself what happened the reader might take a crayon and black out that area. The southern area is what remains of the once-orderly whole.

In the grand design, I judge, the reduction of all Africa to the condition now prevailing in the northern part, so that the whole becomes a vacuum waiting to be filled is held to be the essential next step in the three-phase strategy of which we have seen the first two phases: the League of Nations of unhappy memory, the United Nations of unhallowed present, and The World Organization of repellent future menace.

The southern area contains three territories of stable government and order. The plan in 1966 was evidently to cut out the two areas (the Rhodesian and Portuguese ones) flanking the greatest one, South Africa, on the east and west, and thus to leave South Africa isolated, vulnerable on both flanks, and open to the concluding attempt by blockade or invasion (or blockade *and* invasion) foreseen by the Carnegie Plan.

The Rhodesian resistance unexpectedly held up the great plan on the eastern flank. It was touch and go in April: I remind the reader again of Dr. Salazar's warning: "One more false step . . ."

Then in July the judgment in the South West Africa case foiled the plan on the western flank. Again it was touch and go: "one more false vote" would have tipped the scale.

Thus the great plan failed for the nonce and the conspiratorial groups behind it now must recast their whole strategy for the next attempt. That will take time, and meanwhile the southern African states grow stronger, not alone in themselves but in the minds of folk in the outer world, who begin to understand the justice of their cause and to perceive the nefarious plan through the ubiquitous propaganda.

This is no happy ending, for the One Worlders, in their various guises and disguises, will not desist, but it does mark a tangible improvement in our prospect and opens a more hopeful future. For this the world has to thank the quiet determination of Mr. Ian Smith in Rhodesia, of Dr. Salazar in Portugal, and in particular the exemplary prudence and resolve of Dr. Verwoerd in South Africa. During this perilous time only calm words and few have ever broken the silence from southern Africa. The Pharisaic moralizings and menaces have come from Westminster, New York and Washington, once the homes of measured words and well-weighed actions. There the day of the demagogue has come and that of the statesman has faded.

The world may now hope to see this fateful year of 1966 pass without a war wantonly begun in Africa. It was within "one more false step" of that in April, and if the South West Africa judgment had been other it would have come again to that brink in the late summer or autumn of 1966, for then a deafening clamour would have gone up from the Tower of Babel in New York for another "act of piracy" to be "converted into a legal act of peacemaking"!

Thus the writer of *Insanity Fair* of 1938 finds himself, for the first time, able in 1966 to conclude this second volume of *Insanity Fair* on a more hopeful note, a new and pleasant thing in his experience. "So far and no further", said Mr. Ian Smith in his Independence speech, and the world has been waiting for those words for many, many years. The leaders of Rhodesia and South Africa, by opposing themselves to the sea of sorrows which loomed, have not ended, but staved them off. The world is still a mad one, my masters, but it looks a little better now than it did a year ago.

POSTSCRIPT

The ominous year, 1966, draws to its end and once more, as in 1938, I wonder whether, when this edition appears, it will be an autopsy on things that have happened, instead of the analysis of cause and impending effect which it is meant to be. I have the same sense, now as in 1938, of events quickening and thickening, like swarming stormbirds, towards a dark, lightning-rent horizon, for much has happened since this book was written (March–June 1966) and first appeared (in August 1966).

1918–1939, 21 years; 1945–1966, 21 years. If this should be the appointed time for another human ordeal, the appointment is not with destiny or the fault in our stars. The appointment is man-made, and made in what we call "The West", for there the build-up towards war suddenly accelerated, as by a foot pressed on a pedal, in 1966. If we have not yet had war, it may have been averted only by the Rhodesian stand and the Hague judgment. The unwary, unseeing multitude has during this year been like Charlie Chaplin teetering blindfold on the edge of an abyss: from this simile they may see the precarious plight in which the peoples have been.

The two respites, which seemed so Godsent, have been only respites, as later events have already shown, and the pressure and prodding towards war continue unabated in London and in New York.

Those who today still think of "Moscow" in this context lag behind events, for the shape of these is changing. I might try to make this clear by borrowing the language of filmdom. If "Oscars" or "Academy Awards" were given for conspiratorial performances, Moscow Communism today would at the utmost qualify for the "best *supporting* player" trophy. That for the best *leading* performer would have to go the conspiratorial force which masquerades as "Liberalism", has its particular citadel in the United Nations building in New York, and has gained a monstrous power within and over the British and American governments.

The immediate and direct threat of *war* at this time comes from there, not from Moscow, and folk who look eastward for it look the wrong way. The world revolution has assumed yet another guise, and "Liberalism" today includes Communism. Africa, in today's

155

planning, has been chosen by this conspiratorial power as the starting-point for another war. But Moscow cannot *directly* attack Southern Africa, and if it tried to, even "The West" could hardly emulate Hitler's deed of 1939 and join hands openly with that Communism which it professes to oppose. Indeed, from very shame "The West" would have to march against it.

Therefore, if the Communist plan to destroy ordered government everywhere in Africa is to succeed, "The West" must be given the daggers and make the attack, so that the true origin and motive be concealed. This is what makes the events of July and September of most significant portent. The open, spelt-out menace of war has come from America (not at the wish of the American people, but against it) and the student of events now must look towards New York, not Moscow, if he seek the true shape of coming events.

I recorded earlier that the World Court judgment of July 18 was a beneficent thing which at that moment thwarted the war-plan. I did not know then (what all the world should know now) that three days *before* that judgment the United States Government delivered a message to the South African Government stating that it would feel bound to support United Nations action on the judgment. The only possible inference is that the American Government expected the judgment to go the other way and was threatening coercion. Compared with this, I submit that even Mr. Chamberlain's visit, with his umbrella, to Herr Hitler in 1938, when he ordered a small, harmless, peace-loving country (Czechoslovakia) to surrender to Hitler, becomes of less significance in the history of ignobility.

For this, unprecedented and hitherto unimaginable, action can only be understood in the light of, and cannot be considered separately from the Carnegie Battle Plan against South Africa which I summarized earlier. The Carnegie "Endowment for International Peace" in New York enjoys tax-exemption, presumably because of the peaceful mission expressed in its name, and therefore must be held to be officially subsidized, for the act of remission amounts to that. The funds of which it disposes were used, among other things, for the production of a detailed plan of the invasion of South Africa, published last year. This was described as a plan for "United Nations Collective Measures" against South Africa. In its Note the American Government committed itself to support United Nations collective measures against South Africa!

156

The Carnegie invasion plan says that lesser military powers might well provide the "ground force" of 93,000 troops against South Africa, but that one major power might have to come in for the final showdown. The American Government cannot have been unaware of this document (it was distributed to all representatives at the United Nations) and in its Note, by obvious implication, put itself forward as that "one major power". I do not see that any other inference can be drawn.

The Carnegie invasion plan set a point in time for the attack on South Africa, saying that if the Hague Court ruled against South Africa the American Government would probably support United Nations action "to enforce the ruling". Three days *before* the judgment, the American Government informed Pretoria that it would support United Nations action on the judgment.

The only reasonable deduction from all this is that the "Liberal" forces behind the Carnegie invasion plan were strong enough to have their way inside the American Government. That is as grave a matter, and produces as dangerous a situation, as can be imagined, and from this moment the part which America, under such occult pressures, is to play in all our tomorrows becomes a thing of vital concern to Americans and to the public masses everywhere.

I might try again to make plain what this is all about by using another simile: that of our space-age rockets. Theirs is a three-stage operation, as the veriest teenager knows. At the start the rear section of the rocket, the booster, propels the vehicle upward. At a predetermined point, the booster falls away, mission accomplished, and the middle section of the rocket takes over. When it has done its part, it too falls away, leaving the frontal section to continue under its own power and complete the mission.

So it is with World Government, and in our day, unless God otherwise disposes, we are about to see the third stage of the three-stage operation attempted. The first stage was that of the League of Nations, which fell away. The second stage is that of the United Nations, which is intended (after another war) to fall away, leaving the World Organization to encompass our little globe.

None of these stages could have been achieved without war, and the concluding stage cannot be accomplished without another war. The first war was begun in the name of "destroying Prussian militarism": nothing was then heard of any "league of nations".

157

At that war's end, the great object of it proved to have been the establishment of this "League of Nations" (within a few years Prussian militarism was stronger than ever, and that made the second stage of the operation possible, by ensuring the necessary war).

This second war was begun with the proclaimed object of "destroying dictatorship" and liberating "small nations" enserfed by it. Such ideas were soon discarded and when the war ended the area of dictatorship was far greater than before, merely the name having changed from Fascism to Communism, and several more small nations had been engulfed by it (under President Roosevelt's orders from Yalta). The main purpose of the war proved to have been the establishment of the United Nations in New York whence, in the last few years, has come all the clamour for another war. The bogus, rabble-rousing issue ("slavery" in 1860: "apartheid" now) has been found and will serve until the war begins, if one is in the event achieved: thereafter, it will soon drop from sight.

The reader may now perceive, before any third war begins, what would come of it at the end. Unless he is extremely shortsighted, he may also foresee the nature of the "World Organization" which would, in truth, be the purpose of it.

While the conspiratorial groups in and around the United Nations, heartened by the American Note, continue their outcry for a war to be begun in Africa, their chorus is echoed across the Atlantic at the conferences of "Commonwealth Prime Ministers". There the raging tumult against the "illegal regime in Rhodesia", and the demand for its destruction, never ceases.

Possibly Gilbert and Sullivan, in collaboration with such as Laurel and Hardy, might do justice to these gatherings, in the form which they have taken today. In the group-pictures, ranged around the Monarch, which are a traditional part of these affairs (dating from the time when they *were* in truth meetings of Commonwealth Prime Ministers) the student may entertain himself by picking out, from among the figures surrounding the smiling, bestarred and beordered Queen, those who are present by dint of assassination, murder, violent usurpation, and rule by tommy-gun and one-man-no-vote in general. Credentials of legitimacy, in *this* case, evidently are not required. One "President" in the group is he who a few weeks earlier ejected his rightful President from palace and country by bullet and grenade. Another represents a "Prime Minister" who became so by the murder of his predecessor, who had previously murdered *his* (both in the current year).

Should the gods laugh or weep at these spectacles in London and New York? The moralistic poses which are struck in these assemblies invest them with the hue of a cynical hypocrisy: to me they seem like the attitudinizings of a bogus priest at a mock marriage.

Thus 1966, the year fraught with peril, moves to its end. The World Court judgment vindicated South Africa: now the United Nations moves to elect new judges, in the obvious hope that on a future occasion some new judgment will give the mask of mock-regality to some new warlike undertaking. The judgment vindicated the mandatory Power: promptly, the United Nations declares that the mandate is at an end and that means must be devised to take over South West Africa.

The dying year brings some cause for better hope. The actions, or antics, of the United Nations begin to disillusion and repel ever-growing masses of people, all of whom cannot be fooled all the time. In Africa north of the Zambezi the process of disintegration goes on apace: each week brings some news of chaos and carnage.

By contrast, the stability of the Southern African countries becomes ever plainer to the mass-mind. Three of the newly-independent small African states in the South have shown that they see their future to lie in reliance on the ordered States behind them, the South African, Rhodesian and Portuguese ones.

But the key to the whole issue remains Rhodesia. The "talks" which began in April and still continued in October led many people in the outer world to think that "something would be arranged", but this was a false lull. The deadlock remains absolute. Rhodesia will not surrender its independence, now established for a year. Mr. Wilson, in London, still avows that if Rhodesia will not yield he will let the United Nations take over. What that would mean, all now know: renewed clamour for war.

On the outcome still depends much more than the independence of Rhodesia. If Rhodesia survives the strength and stability of Southern Africa will gradually effect an improvement in the now-disintegrating North, and therewith a return to stability in Africa as a whole. If Rhodesia falls, the move for war against South Africa will immediately gain momentum in New York, and in the

159

sequel to that the multitudes of people far away, who have no immediate concern with Africa or any interest in its ruination, will find themselves drawn as into a vortex.

There has been a false lull, in these mid-year months of 1966, but the decision has yet to come, and now impends.

INTERVIEW WITH MR. IAN SMITH

Ten months after the Declaration of Independence, when this book had already appeared in Southern Africa and was going to press in the United States, I sought an opportunity to learn Mr. Ian Smith's feeling about the dramatic events of these months and about the future prospect. I expressed my admiration of the stand taken by Rhodesia under his leadership and my own conviction that it was just and right and historically of major importance for the future of Africa and of the world: this was the conviction that originally brought me to Rhodesia to tell the tale of Independence, and I recalled that when I arrived, early in the year 1966, the issue seemed very much to hang on a razor's edge. Prudence and firmness, I thought, had vindicated themselves, and the outlook, though still unclear, was, in my opinion, a good deal better now than then.

"Can you tell me, Prime Minister," I said, "what shape the events of the last nine months now have in your mind?"

"The most significant factor that comes to my mind," he said, "is the way in which we have created a Rhodesian nation; a nation which is strong, courageous and determined to maintain a civilization in Rhodesia based on Christian teachings and ideals. I have also been tremendously impressed at the unanimity of resolution amongst all Rhodesians, ranging from our children at school, at the one end, right through to our aged people at the other."

"Yes, that is the picture I have gained," I said, "and how do you now see the future development of the matter."

"At the moment we are holding talks with the British Government," Mr. Smith replied, "and much depends on the outcome of these. It is difficult to prognosticate on how these talks will end but I can say that Rhodesia is prepared for any eventuality."

Then I expressed my personal view, as a political observer and writer, that the real object of the actions taken by "the Wets" in 1966 was South Africa. The intention as I saw it, I said, was to "pinch out" the hindrances on South Africa's eastern and western flanks, namely, Rhodesia and South West Africa, and thus leave South Africa isolated, open and vulnerable to concerted action by blockade, in order to force the change in South African domestic policy to which the groups operating in the name of "the West" were committed. I asked the Prime Minister if he felt able to express an opinion about this.

He said: "Your reasoning that South Africa is the ultimate target seems to me to be sound and logical. I believe that the reasons for Rhodesia's stand are clear for all the world to see—the forces of Communism—this is what makes the actions of the Western nations seem more incredible."

Again expressing my own view, I said I thought that this "pincer movement" had been blunted by (1) the successful Rhodesian resistance, and (2) the judgment in the South West African case. I recalled that in the early stages of the Rhodesian blockade Dr. Salazar of Portugal had given warning against "one more false step" that might set the world ablaze, and hazarded my own opinion that in July "one more false vote" might have brought similar dangers with it. Again, I asked whether Mr. Ian Smith cared to comment on this, my reading of events.

"Again I cannot but agree with the thoughts that you have expressed," he answered.

I said that I thought the term "liberalism" had in our century lost its original meaning and was now a cover-name for all manner of dangerous plans and plots, and that I hoped this was beginning to dawn on the mind of the public masses. In this respect, I thought the resistance of Rhodesia had played an invaluable part in awakening large bodies of opinion overseas. Did he care to say anything about that?

"There is no doubt in my mind," said Mr. Ian Smith, "that liberalism is being used as a cover by the Communists to further their own political ideologies. Communism, as you know, is a creed which has tremendous appeal to the 'have nots'. The fact that those who have anything in this world have obtained what they have through their own initiative, enterprise, ability, skill—in other words, on merit—is quietly pushed out of the way."

"Do you, Prime Minister," I asked, "feel able at this stage to say anything about the future prospect of 'The Talks'?"

He smiled. "I am always optimistic," he said. "More than that I do not believe I should say at this stage."

Among many reports, I said, was a recent one to the effect that

Mr. Harold Wilson, who could no longer believe in the efficacy of sanctions, contemplated throwing the matter into the hands of the United Nations. In my own view, I said, I could hardly credit that he would do this, after the experience of earlier months leading up to the moment of Dr. Salazar's one more false step warning. What could Mr. Smith say, if anything, on this point?

He considered. Then, "I find it difficult," he answered, "to predict Mr. Wilson's actions. However, I do not believe that he would wish to hand this matter over to the United Nations, for two reasons—firstly, this would be a desperate gesture which would probably aggravate the position for both Britain and Rhodesia; secondly, by so doing, Mr. Wilson would be going back on much of what he has said to date. This would be tantamount to conceding defeat on the Rhodesian question. I am doubtful whether Mr. Wilson would be prepared to do this."

I ended by expressing again the admiration I felt, as an Englishman, for the stand taken by Mr. Ian Smith and the Rhodesian Government at a moment when, in my judgment, capitulation would have had the effect of spreading into the last remaining stable area of Africa the condition of chaos and carnage now rife in the north. I recalled the phrase in Mr. Ian Smith's Independence speech which shook me out of my resolve never again to write about political things, and said how glad I was to have been a witness of the siege of Salisbury. From the time of Mr. Stanley Baldwin and Mr. Neville Chamberlain, I said, true men everywhere had been waiting to hear the words, "So far and no further!" and at last they had come from the place where the Pioneer Column outspanned and Cecil Rhodes built his home. It would always be a happy memory to me to have come into the act at this late and, in my opinion, happier stage.

I left Mr. Ian Smith as I first found him, calm, unhurried, imperturbably courteous and quietly resolved. Looking back on my life's experience as a writer, and witness of so many years of abdication and retreat in the West, I wished him and his country, from my heart, and for the good of all men, success in their memorable stand.

POLITICAL ASSASSINATION

I said earlier that during the years when I wrote nothing I forgot much of what I had written. A friend reminded me of something I wrote in my book *Far and Wide* (published in 1951), which I had forgotten, and I re-read it with feelings of growing interest and surprise.

At that time (1949) I was led, by a visit to the Ford Theatre in Washington, to study the circumstances of President Lincoln's murder and, proceeding from that, to make some study of political assassination in general. I found (with Mr. Truslow Adams) that investigation never uncovers the deep background of such deeds, and that they are recurrently disposed of with the explanation "madman", whereas all signs point to thorough organization based on long experience.

Re-reading that chapter, I was astonished to find how closely it fits the circumstances of Dr. Verwoerd's assassination, and, what is more, how remarkably similar the background to the murder was in *both* cases. By substituting the word "apartheid" for "slavery" and "Verwoerd" for "Lincoln" in that chapter* an almost identical picture of the backgrounds, underlying motives and hoped-for consequences may be obtained, in both cases. The background to President Lincoln's murder, as I reconstructed it in 1949 from the annals and my own observations, is to my mind identical with the situation in today's America, where the same bogus issue (apartheid: slavery) is being used to inflame passions (against "the South" then: against South Africa now) in the direction of a wanton war, which could only lead to "a sea of infamy and misery" (Mr. Truslow Adams).

I find the eight pages I then wrote so apposite to today's state of affairs, particularly as it has been shaped by the destruction of Dr. Verwoerd that I asked the publisher to reproduce it as an appendix to this book.

---

*"Of Murder and Motive", *Far and Wide*, published 1951 by Jonathan Cape, London.

OF MURDER AND MOTIVE

. . . This mystery has four chief parts: the man, the moment, the murderers and the motive.

The man, like the victims of other comparable crimes, was a unifier and reconciler. He fought the South to preserve the Union, *not* to abolish slavery: "My paramount object is not to save or destroy slavery . . . If all earthly powers were given me I should not know what to do with the existing institution" (of slavery). Though he unwillingly issued the slave-freeing Proclamation he never departed in conviction from the original, declared aim of the war: "It is not for any purpose . . . of interfering with the rights or established institutions of the Secession States but to preserve the Union with all the dignity, equality and rights of the several States unimpaired." He intended to defeat only the claimed right to secede;* then to restore the Union and leave the legal institution of slavery to be gradually modified into abolition by judicial courts.

In that policy the Leftist Republicans around him saw the danger of the conservative Democrats returning to power. They introduced the false issue of slavery into the war to perpetuate the Republican Party in power by taking the vote from the Southern States and the Southern whites and giving it to the negroes, of whom not one in a hundred could then read. (Similarly the aims of the Second World War, when it was half run, were changed from the liberation of countries overrun and the restoration of parliamentary governments to "the defeat of Fascism", which meant their re-surrender to Soviet Communism.)

Lincoln's Republican Party contained the mass of Leftists, who were near to dominating it. Lincoln knew that they raised the bogus issue to inflame passions and prolong the war; his own Secretary of War, Edwin Stanton (who with Thaddeus Stevens headed this group), said so: "The great aim of the war is to abolish slavery. To end the war before the nation is ready for that would be a failure.

---

*The secession dispute itself is one of history's recurrent jests, summed up by an American humorist in these words: "If you admit the right of secession, sir, my sympathies are with the South; if you deny it, God bless his Majesty!"

The war must be prolonged and conducted so as to achieve that."
(The Second World War was similarly prolonged, through wasteful
detours, to achieve "the defeat of Fascism", but *not* the original aim.)
Lincoln was an obstacle to the forces of destruction in his own party.

Such was the *man*. The *moment* of his murder was that at which he
was about to fulfil his policy of reconciliation and accomplish the
declared aim of the war. Two days before Lee at last surrendered
and Washington was lit up. At the very moment Lincoln's emissary,
General Sherman, was negotiating with the Southern leaders a truce
following Lincoln's constant line: no confiscation or political disable-
ment, recognition of the Southern States governments if they took
the oath to the Constitution, reunion, conciliation. (That was as if
President Roosevelt, at Yalta, had upheld the war aims originally
understood by the Western peoples, instead of surrendering half of
Europe to a regime resembling that endured by the South after
Lincoln's death.) At Lincoln's last cabinet meeting, on the day he
was killed, he said he was glad Congress was adjourned; the
extremists in it would not be able to hinder the work of reviving
State governments in orderly fashion. "There must be no bloody
work", he would have no part in hangings or killings; the task was
"to extinguish resentments".

At that moment the man was killed. In the choice of time and
victim the crime startlingly resembles four others, which also struck
down unifiers and conciliators just when they seemed likely to
impede the process of universal revolutionary destruction. Alexander II of Russia emancipated twenty million serfs in 1861 and
pursued his work of reconciliation until he was murdered in 1881;
of that crime Soviet Communism and Political Zionism were born.
In 1913 the Archduke was killed at Serajevo; he had the reputation
of a unifier and conciliator who might have saved the Austro-
Hungarian Empire from war and disintegration, *had he lived*. In 1934
Alexander of Yugoslavia was killed at Marseilles; he was a unifier
who could not have been turned from his throne by an ally, as his
little-known eighteen-year-old son Peter was in effect in 1945 by
Mr. Churchill, and a Communist dictator set in his place. In 1948
Count Bernadotte was murdered as he completed a plan of truce
and pacification in Palestine.

Each of these events changed the course of history for the worse.
Together with the wars and annexations to which they led and the

revolutionary movements which profited by them, they produced the state of affairs with which the Western world finds itself faced at this mid-century. In each case the men marked for death were ones who stood for reconciliation, unity, orderly judicial reforms and "the extinguishing of resentments", as Lincoln said. In each instance (save that of Count Bernadotte, where no pretence of justice was done), nondescript individuals were publicly presented as the culprits. On each occasion a powerful organization obviously stood behind those puppets and each time all was done to prevent its exposure.

None can doubt today that Lincoln was removed to prevent the reconciliation of North and South and the consolidation of the Union. Though the wound did seem later to heal, the events of today show it still te be raw, so that the conspirators' aim of 1865 cannot yet be said, in 1950, to have failed. Time has yet to show this result, with all others.

The culprits displayed to the populace were the usual group of obscure individuals, who clearly could not have carried out the deed unaided. Lincoln's killer, the actor John Wilkes Booth, escaped for a while. A benchful of generals promptly executed one Lewis Paine,* a youth called David Herold who accompanied Booth in his flight, a mysterious German, George Atzerodt, and a woman boarding-housekeeper, Mrs. Suratt. Pending trial, the prisoners were kept in solitary cells, with empty cells on either side, and made to wear thick padded hoods, with small holes for nose and mouth, over head and shoulders. The only plausible explanation is that communication with any other person whatsoever was to be prevented. These four, and four men sent to a remote island, all *knew* Booth and his associates. Men who helped him escape, but did not know him before, were not even charged.

That looks as if the capital offence was to be in possession of information about Booth's movements and acquaintances in Washington. For that the State prosecutor seems to have demanded death and the four men sent to an island only escaped it because the generals shied at wholesale hangings without evidence of complicity. Studying this aspect of the matter, I recalled van der Lubbe, the vagrant found in the burning Reichstag. I believe he was kept

---

*Who simultaneously attacked, but did not kill, the Secretary of State, Frederick Seward, the only other man in Lincoln's Cabinet who unfalteringly pursued reunion and reconciliation.

drugged during his trial and until his beheading; he alone could have said who put him in the Reichstag. The demeanour of Rudolf Hess, at the Nuremberg Trial, was similar to that of van der Lubbe; none but he could publicly explain the wartime mission on which he was sent to England.

The circumstances of Lincoln's murder speak for themselves. Booth fired the shot into his neck as he watched the play. The door of the box was unlocked, but on the inner side of it someone had placed a wooden bar and a mortice, so that Booth could ensure that none entered it *after* himself! At the door should have been Lincoln's armed bodyguard, a Washington policeman, recently enlisted, called John F. Parker. Only his empty chair was there and no word survives in the records to say why he was not in it! This collapse of protective vigilance was a feature of the Serajevo, Marseilles and Jerusalem murders. President Lincoln's danger was well known. That very afternoon he asked his Secretary of War if Stanton's stalwart aide, a Major Eckert, could accompany him to the theatre for his protection. Stanton refused and Eckert, asked by the President himself, also declined (on the next day Stanton telegraphed to General Sherman that he too was in danger "and I beseech you to be more heedful than Mr. Lincoln was of such knowledge").

The missing bodyguard, Parker, was appointed less than a fortnight before the murder, during Lincoln's absence from Washington, so that the usual presidential confirmation of his appointment was never obtained. In three years service serious complaints of "neglect of duty" were several times made against him and in April 1864 he was dismissed. In December 1864 he was reinstated and in April 1865, immediately before the deed, allotted to the President's personal protection! After the murder he was again charged with "neglect of duty"; the trial was secret, the complaint was dismissed, and the records of the hearing have vanished from the files. Three years later he was once again charged with dereliction, dismissed, and at that point vanishes from history!

Thus Booth walked into an unguarded box, shot the President, jumped on to the stage, ran through unguarded wings to the back door, jumped on a waiting horse and rode away. He caught his spurred boot on some bunting as he jumped, fell awkwardly and broke a small bone in his leg.

This alone seems to have prevented him from getting clean away.

He rode across the Anacostia bridge and along the well-known route to Virginia which the Southerners, throughout the war, used for spies and communications with the North. Behind him galloping cavalrymen were sent to scour the country, north and west, which he obviously would avoid. This one southward route, which a flying Southerner would clearly take, was left open long enough for him to escape. His unforeseeable injury prevented that; unable to go on the actor went into hiding.

If his escape was desired, this naturally threw up a new problem. After a few days his whereabouts became known and the chase was converging on him when the military Provost Marshal, who led it, was suddenly recalled to Washington and the pursuit entrusted to the head of the secret service, one Colonel Lafayette C. Baker. He was given "twenty-six cavalrymen" commanded by "a reliable and discreet commissioned officer", Lieutenant Doherty. This officer, however, was placed under the orders of two of Colonel Baker's detectives, his cousin, ex-Lieutenant Luther B. Baker, and an ex-Colonel Conger, who "by courtesy was conceded the command". Whose courtesy is not recorded, though Lieutenant Doherty's chagrin is. This force eventually surrounded the barn where Booth lay hidden, with strict orders to take him alive. Of the twenty-nine men none could clearly say later who fired the shot which killed him. Baker thought Conger did; Conger denied it.

Clearly Booth would have escaped but for his damaged foot. With his death none remained who could tell the whole truth; those who knew most were quickly hanged or exiled.

Thus the *man*, the *moment*, and the *apparent murderers*. The *motive* today seems as clear as the organization behind it remained, and remains, obscure. It was to remove Lincoln because he was an obstacle to the destruction of the South. The student from afar, who finds Lincoln honoured equally with Washington, on deeper study learns how lonely he was when he died. To the collapsing South he was the destroyer; to the North he was the enemy of further destruction. Today's traveller may perceive a great flaw in the array of memorials erected to Lincoln in his country. Suggestively, they commemorate his as the slayer of slavery, first and foremost. It is the continuation of a falsehood; that was not his primary aim, he was against violent demagogic actions, preferred judicial gradualness, and had at heart only the unity of the Union. Thus his memory

169

is misused today in the further pursuit of ulterior schemes; the false issue, the falsity of which he saw, is raised in his name and his words and monuments are presented as its also.

In the South the news was received as a last unaccountable blow of destiny. In the North different feelings were expressed. Clerics, frequently thirsty for a vengeance claimed by God, avowed that the deed must be a divine act, albeit mysteriously performed. A Republican Congressman, Mr. George Julian, later recalled that his party met the day after the murder "to consider a line of policy less conciliatory than that of Mr. Lincoln"; while everybody was shocked the feeling of the meeting was overwhelmingly that the accession of a new President "would prove a Godsend to the country".

Mr. Truslow Adams's *Epic* dismisses "the conspiracy of a handful, led by a half-madman, which destroyed the one man who stood between his country and the powers of evil and plunged us all into a sea of infamy and misery". The description of the deed and its effects is accurate, but the theory of the recurrent madman grows thin. Coincidence did not drop Gavrile Princep at the spot where he could kill the Archduke, Vlada the Chauffeur into a Marseilles street as King Alexander went by, and the deadbeat van der Lubbe into the Reichstag (I saw him and his trial and can vouch for that). Even if coincidence's arm were so long, it could not always reach to the suppression of inquiry in these cases.

This is a chapter by itself in our times, and in my opinion the most important. I remember how governments combined, at the League of Nations in 1935, to shelve the inquiry into the complicity of other governments in the murder of King Alexander. The same thing happened in the case of Count Bernadotte; the United Nations dropped the matter of its own emissary's murder as if it were a hot coal. The truth is not, as American writers put it, that "history shrinks" from exposing these things. Politicians recurrently cover them up and conceal the continuing process.The study of Lincoln's murder did more than anything hitherto to convince me that it *is* a continuing process, with an enduring organization behind it. It shares identical and recognizable features with the later series of murders, which all led to the spread of the area of destruction. These conspiracies cannot be improvised; obviously the experience of generations, or centuries, lies in the choice of moment, method, line of retreat and concealment. The little folk who are trotted out after each such deed may be "the handful", but the hand is never seen. Particularly in this matter of covering-up is Lincoln's murder of present-day significance in America. The same resolute and efficient methods are used to defeat public curiosity about Communist infiltration into government departments, the public services and high places. In America (and for that matter in England and Canada), a cat sometimes slips out of the bag, a Dr. May, a Dr. Fuchs, a Mr. Alger Hiss. But then the bag is tied more tightly than before, and the public mind forgets.

Booth was not a madman. He kept a diary and the entries he made while he lay hidden show a sane man, even though pages were apparently removed before its existence became known, two years after it was taken from his body! He wrote among other things, "I have almost a mind to return to Washington and in a measure clear my name, which I feel I can do" (the anonymous bullet effectively prevented his return to Washington). A Congressman asked, "How clear himself? By disclosing his accomplices?" A parliamentary commission also set about to find who were the persons "many of them holding high positions of power and authority . . . who acted through inferior persons who were their tools and accomplices". Nothing much came of that in 1865, or of similar efforts in 1950.

Among high persons of that time the eye of today's curiosity falls chiefly on Edwin Stanton. As Secretary of War in a country at war he was almost supremely powerful. All communications were under his personal censorship. All acts tending to deflect Booth's pursuit, or after Booth's death to obscure the trail, seem traceable to him and the Leftists around him. Within a few hours of the murder he wrote to the American Minister in London of "evidence obtained" to show that the murder was "deliberately planned and set on foot by rebels, under pretence of avenging the South". Just so did Goering claim to have proof that Communists fired the Reichstag, while it still burned. Stanton may have pictured himself as dictator; he nearly achieved such status in the sequel of events. He forced through Congress a Reconstruction Bill to dissolve the Southern States and degrade them to military districts, and a Tenure of Office Bill framed to deprive the new President of the constitutional power to dismiss himself, Stanton. When President Johnson did dismiss him he refused to resign and only failed by one Senator's vote to secure the President's impeachment. Andrew Johnson proved a stauncher man than the Leftists expected when he succeeded Lincoln. Among the most arresting questions of American history is, what would have ensued had Johnson's impeachment succeeded by one vote, not failed. Since President Roosevelt revived the political issues of Reconstruction days the conundrum has gained new and current interest.

Sitting at my restaurant window I pictured Booth riding away from Ford's Theatre. "There you go," I thought, "Wilkes Booth, Gavrile Princep, Marinus van der Lubbe, Vlada the Chauffeur: whatever your name, your unimportant shape is clear, but the darkness around you hides your masters . . ."